FLAT
SWITZERLAND
A FUN CYCLING GUIDE

KATRIN GYGAX

FLAT SWITZERLAND

A FUN CYCLING GUIDE

TABLE OF CONTENTS

WELCOME TO FLAT SWITZERLAND!

I've used Swiss trains as my office every summer since 2009, spending my lunch hours riding around the Alps on my bicycle. And I mean *around*, not *over*. I cycle from one Swiss town to another, leaving my bike behind and picking it up again at a later date to ride it to the next destination. By the end of the season, I've usually completed my own kind of Tour de Suisse. The best part: I don't have to push myself up any busy mountain passes. Because around the Alps, Switzerland is flat. It's amazingly flat, if you know where to look.

But it's not about being lazy. *Flat Switzerland* is a guide for those who would love to cycle Switzerland the slow tourism way. Who want to see the whole country, well away from loud roads packed with cars and motorcycles zooming past in high gear. From the gentle routes of this book, you'll be able to really take in the entire Swiss landscape – including the Alps.

Picture yourself gliding at a leisurely pace through the country's celebrated cow-bearing fields, along sapphire rivers and emerald lakes, often on paths open only to walkers, farming vehicles and you. The sights are quieter, you're aware of more details. And there's time to enjoy them.

Stop at one of Switzerland's famous red benches along the trail and contemplate a hawk circling his lunch above a nearby meadow; read a book, have a sandwich or watch a river flow by on its way out to the Mediterranean.

Notice how architecture can change with the local dialect – which might switch languages from one village to another and then unexpectedly shift back in the next.

Come upon wonderful surprises, like outwardly unassuming churches festooned with fantastic beasts carved into stone, astonishing murals and pastel wedding-cake colors speckled with gold.

Pull into the outdoor terrace of a 300-year-old chalet-turned-restaurant and enjoy a sumptuous lunch under a blue sky. Visit a local farm store, cheese shop, butcher or bakery to get supplies for a picnic by the lake. Take along a cooling bag for spontaneous purchases. Bring home fresh strawberries, wild garlic bratwurst or blue melilot cheese to make the memories of your trip last a little longer.

And instead of sticky (and stinky) racing Lycra, you can do all of this in airy, comfortable clothing – and in shoes you can actually walk in when you get off your bike.

Welcome to Flat Switzerland, where you'll finally have time to enjoy yourself!

Katrin Gygax

INTRODUCTION

THE FINE PRINT

Most of these cycling stages follow Switzerland's official national routes – look for the red "SchweizMobil/ SuisseMobile/SvizzeraMobile" signs at the train station and at route intersections. But sometimes they will veer off along quieter country lanes or even flatter shortcuts, so make sure to read through the route description section of the one you want to take.

A GPX or KML map for each route can be downloaded from flatswitzerland.com/routes

Due to the nature of the global positioning system and depending on the quality of your cell phone reception at any given point, the ascent, descent, kilometrage and your exact location on the road may vary slightly.

A study by the non-profit Institute of Navigation (ion. org) found smartphones to be accurate within a 4.9 meter radius, a value that can increase near trees or narrow valleys.

Sights indicated with kilometrage are measured from the starting point listed on the first page of the route – usually directly outside the train station. Check websites for details on sights before you go and remember: URLs can change, which is why I've left things simple. Nothing worse than a broken link. In smaller towns, tourism websites may be available only in German, French or Italian. In that case, go to myswitzerland.com, pick your language and type in the name of the town you're looking for.

Getting your bike onto the train can be a chore depending on the time of day and year you're traveling. Although Swiss Rail (SBB) includes slots for bicycles on its trains, you may need to reserve a space ahead of time (InterCity trains) or find them occupied by luggage. Reserve a bike slot at sbb.ch or in the SBB app.

Think about renting a bike. Hotels often offer bikes for rent or even free use. Rentabike.ch has a network throughout Switzerland and is partnered with SBB, so you can do one-way rentals. Also, if you do need to take these rented bikes onto a train, they ride for free (a plus if you've decided to skip part of a route or get a quick boost to the next one).

You can combine the following routes into multiday tours, or spread them out over the spring-to-early-fall season for one big tour de Suisse. I recommend saving Chur–Sargans for the fall wine tastings.
- Stein–Basel–France–Basel Circle
- Aarau–Olten–Solothurn–Biel–Neuchâtel–Yverdon
- Lausanne–Montreux–Aigle–Martigny–Sion–Sierre–Leuk–Brig
- Kandersteg–Spiez–Interlaken
- Brünig–Sarnen–Luzern–Zug–Zurich
- Chur–Sargans–St. Margrethen

If you get a flat tire and the nearest bike shop is closed, look for an inner tube vending machine outside its premises. Better yet, take along a canister of tire spray, which reinflates your tire with a mix of air and glue, closing the leak at the same time (make sure your bike's tires have the air valves to match).

How to cycle a roundabout. If you're new to Switzerland or do not have much experience cycling in traffic, riding in a roundabout may make you nervous. But it's not as terrifying as it may seem. The trick is to be aware of the rules and keep an eye on what everyone else is doing. The most important point as a cyclist is to ride in the middle of the lane, so that cars behind you can't pass you (they aren't allowed to). This keeps the traffic calm and prevents accidents. The driver behind you may get irritated, but that's their problem because you are obeying the law.

Traffic regulations dictate the following for roundabouts:
- every vehicle must slow down before entering the roundabout
- all traffic coming from the left has the right of way
- bicycles must drive in the middle of the lane and may not overtake each other
- if there are two lanes within the roundabout, stay in the middle of the right lane
- you must signal before you exit the roundabout
- watch out for pedestrian crossings immediately outside the roundabout

©swissdrone

MAKING FIRES IN SWITZERLAND

While researching this chapter, I put "grilling in Switzerland" into Google Search and got these suggestions in the "People also ask" feature:
- Is grilling popular in Europe?
- Can I use a BBQ on my balcony?
- What is the most popular holiday for grilling?
- Can I have a gas BBQ on my balcony?

Which to me reads like a little story of preparation (I'm going to Europe and don't want to look stupid if I bring my grill), budget (I'll be in an apartment, no way can I afford a house in Switzerland), stealth (if I'm going to smoke out the neighborhood, better do it when everyone else is) and strategy (gas BBQs make less smoke).

Intrigued, and because I knew this book would be issued in German and French as well, I entered:

"Barbecue en Suisse", which gave me (in French):
- Which barbecue on a balcony?
- Can I have a barbecue on my terrace?
- Where can I barbecue on Lake Geneva?
- Which barbecue is allowed?

"Grillieren in der Schweiz" and got (in German):
- Is grilling allowed Switzerland?
- Where is it forbidden to barbecue?
- Is barbecuing allowed in the forest?
- When is it forbidden to barbecue?

From which I deduce that while the Romands are interested in quality authorized equipment and being considerate of their neighbors – and seem to be clustered around Lake Geneva – German-speakers have made up their mind that a BBQ is going to happen, they just don't want to get arrested doing it.

There is no federal law against making fires outdoors in Switzerland and the Swiss Civil Code gives everyone the right to access forests, even privately owned ones. Cantons and municipalities may have specific regulations, such as for nature reserves, or temporary measures, like during times of drought (these may even be permanent, depending on the region). You should therefore always check regional restrictions ahead of time. Local municipalities often post signs informing you when making fires is not permitted.

Do not make fires! Risk of forest fires

The Federal Office for the Environment has a website (in German, French, Italian and English) that shows you which regions are currently at risk for forest fires: waldbrandgefahr.ch

If grilling is allowed, and you don't come across an official fire pit, your number one priority is to make sure your fire doesn't get out of control. Only plan to make a fire large enough for what you're going to cook, and before lighting it, fashion a stable ring of large stones around it, with a clear area beyond the stones. Always ensure the fire is completely extinguished before you leave.

The safest way to have a barbecue outdoors is to use official public fire pits, which can be found all over Switzerland. So what's an "official" fire pit? Although there is no general rule, you can consider it authorized by local authorities if there is at least one bench and a professionally constructed ring of large stones around the center. Often there is a built-in grate and a garbage can nearby. You may even find a woodpile, a water pipe or a picnic area that might include a roof or be inside a hut. A full-on barbecue spot is often in a park with a playground nearby. Official public fire pits close to our routes are included in each chapter.

The family magazine *Schweizer Familie* sponsors and maintains almost 600 fire pits all around the country. Each one has their plaque affixed to it and their schweizerfeuerstellen.ch website lists the infrastructure of each one.

If you don't know whether there will be a woodpile, think about how much fire you're really going to need. It bears repeating: keep it small. A bonfire may even be illegal in the municipality you're in. You can either forage for wood or bring some with you. One or two small logs, some kindling and a newspaper is enough for a few sausages or apples at the end of sticks. Don't forget the matches.

Most importantly, remember to bring water to extinguish your fire when you're done, or a container to scoop water from the nearby river or lake, if there is one. And don't make a fire at all if the wind is too strong.

BADIS AND CAMPGROUNDS

The *Badeanstalt* (literally "bathing establishment") or *lido* is one word for what needs three in English – parks next to a lake or river, beaches or pools. (French divides the *Badi* into pools (*piscines*) or beaches (*plages*)). The concept arose out of a combination of historical events. The Romans arrived in what was to become Switzerland in the 1st century BCE, bringing with them the concept of baths for the general public, as evidenced at archeological sites all over the country (Augusta Raurica, Vindonissa, below the Château de Colombier, under Thermengasse in Zurich). Some of these baths remained in use long after the Romans officially left in the 5th century CE, and even though they eventually crumbled or were built over, the idea of enclosed baths took hold, also thanks to the many natural thermal springs within Switzerland.

Frauenbadi
Zurich

Reformation leaders frowned upon the practice of bathing in front of one's neighbors, with its perceived potential for unchastity, so keeping oneself clean was moved to outdoor fountains under cover of night, as well as indoors to bedrooms stocked with a pitcher and bowl for quick "cat-baths", or to private tubs for the wealthy.

With industrialization came increased water consumption, and the water quality in new pipe networks soon became a problem. As a result, hygiene was now classified as more important than religious Puritanism and *Badis* were built along rivers and lakeshores, although men's and women's sections were safely segregated. These *Badis* have evolved into today's multi-use venues for swimming, relaxing in the sun and family gatherings. Many include saunas, beach volleyballs courts and minigolf courses. Two things to note to stay safe: swimming off boat piers is not permitted, and as opposed to *Badis* that charge admission, free ones don't always have a lifeguard.

Seebad
Luzern

Badis often have either a restaurant, self-serve cafeteria or at least a snack bar attached that is open to non-visitors. Like the English pub or the American diner, the Swiss cafeteria can be relied on to offer certain staples: grilled sausages; French fries; some sort of neutralized pasta; salad with "French" or "Italian" dressing. They sometimes reflect local tastes (real fettucine in Ticino, *Älplermagrone* in Graubünden), but you'll pretty much know what to expect. These days, some cafeterias are making an effort to offer better quality ingredients, while others have added international items that are still essentially junk food, but reflect modern tastes: burgers, hot dogs and döners.

Swiss campgrounds are often located on the lakeshore or riverside and combined with a *Badi*. Where in other countries the camping spots may be empty until a guest comes and parks their recreational vehicle or pitches their tent on it, in Switzerland many spaces may already be filled with stationary trailers for rent and tents can be in the minority. Trailers may also be surrounded by fencing and have porches added to them for a more permanent look. These days, campgrounds can also include a series of small wooden cabins for rent.

Campgrounds are often destinations for families who come every year – even booking the same trailer each time – turning them into small resorts for those on a smaller budget.

ROUTES

CHUR–SARGANS

Wine & Rhine

GRAUBÜNDEN,
ST. GALLEN

SIGHTS

Chur, Rhine, Bündner Herrschaft wine region, Heididorf, Bad Ragaz, Tamina Gorge

FOOD

cafés, restaurants, freeway rest area, fire pit, picnic areas

SPECIALTIES

award-winning wines from 70 different vintners

SWIMMING

Rhine; Hallenbad Obere Au and Freibad Sand in Chur; thermal baths in Bad Ragaz

HOTELS

all ranges in Chur; small historical hotels, B&Bs and "sleep barrels" in Malans, Jenins, Maienfeld and Fläsch; all ranges and luxury resorts in Bad Ragaz, limited in Sargan

 START

Chur

 FINISH

Sargans

 DISTANCE

29.23 km

 ELEVATION GAIN

-103 m

 ASCENT

98 m

 DESCENT

201 m

 KID–FRIENDLY

yes

 TOURISM

chur.graubuenden.ch

heidiland.com

GPX TRACK

Flat Switzerland 1

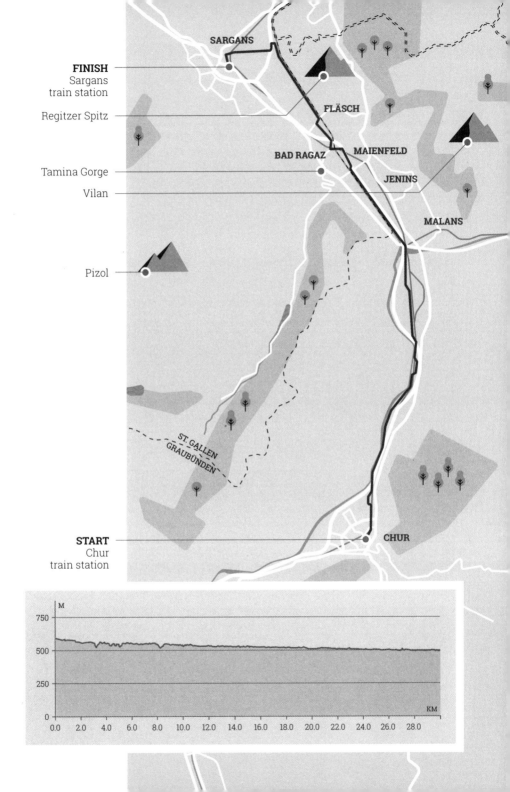

SARGANS

FINISH
Sargans
train station

Regitzer Spitz

FLÄSCH

MAIENFELD

Tamina Gorge

BAD RAGAZ

Vilan

JENINS

MALANS

Pizol

ST. GALLEN
GRAUBÜNDEN

START
Chur
train station

CHUR

M

750

500

250

0

0.0   2.0   4.0   6.0   8.0   10.0   12.0   14.0   16.0   18.0   20.0   22.0   24.0   26.0   28.0

KM

Route description

Glide down the calmer, tree-lined beginnings of the Rhine along the foot of the Calanda Massif, through the historical Bündner Herrschaft wine region to Sargans, where the river widens considerably as it makes a hard right on its way to Lake Constance. This route is a great excuse to do some wine-tasting – just add a side trip up the hill to Malans, Jenins, Maienfeld or Fläsch. With all the things to do along the way, it's worth turning it into a two or three-day getaway.

Rodauen
Woods

At the Chur train station, turn left along Bahnhofplatz to Alexanderstrasse, then cross Gürtelstrasse – where the name of the street you're on changes to Stampastrasse – and join national cycling route #2 to Landquart. Past the Landquart train station but before the river, switch to #21 to Sargans. This route follows the freeway for about 6 km. Noise-cancelling headphones may come in handy. Or you might want to try out some full blast, out-loud singing. You will disturb no one except perhaps your fellow cyclists.

Just past Maienfeld, behind the Heidiland freeway rest area, cross the Rhine over the railway bridge. Turn right onto Rheindammstrasse, which runs along the top of the left dike of the Rhine. If you miss that turn (it's easy to do) no problem: take the next right onto Rheinstrasse to Heulösergangstrasse, which comes to an end at Rheinaustrasse. Turn right there and a few hundred meters later you'll meet up with Rheindammstrasse again. Turn left. After 4 km, keep an eye out for the red #21 sign on your left, pointing you along another Rheinaustrasse through the fields to the Sargans train station.

Bündner Herrschaft

Along the way

As Switzerland's oldest city, Chur has a nice medieval center. Highlights include an 800-year-old cathedral and an episcopal court that dates back to Roman times. Past Landquart lie the sloped vineyards of Malans, Jenins, Maienfeld and Fläsch in the Bündner Herrschaft. They are well worth a detour.

Maienfeld is of course also the setting of the children's book *Heidi*, which is reflected in many ways throughout the area (a tour of the Heididorf is fun for kids).

Further down the road, the thermal baths and spas of Bad Ragaz offer luxurious relaxation; the shaded trail to the Tamina Gorge provides a cool (in both senses of the word) one-hour walk.

Swiss cuisine abounds in Chur's old town and in the wineries of the Bündner Herrschaft. This is a good place for a *Bündnerplatte*, a platter of selected charcuterie, cheeses and pickled vegetables.

The Rheinau picnic area in the woods off to the left (24.9 km) on yet another Rheinaustrasse has three grated public fire pits, with benches, wood, garbage cans and water provided.

There are large and small supermarkets in all the towns; the Landquart Fashion Outlet offers take-out; the Maienfeld station has a kiosk and a vending machine for Sunday snack emergencies; and the Heidiland freeway rest area has a "back door" for cyclists and hikers.

The wines of the Bündner Herrschaft make fall the best time to visit Malans, Jenins, Maienfeld and Fläsch. Check the tourism website for details. There are tastings all over and if you are hit by a desire to take a drop or two home, no worries: the wine merchants all deliver.

The Rhine outside Sargans

Swimming options look obvious: the Rhine is everywhere. But be careful of strong currents and cold water, depending on the time of year. Bad Ragaz is at the other end of the spectrum: its famous hotels have various thermal baths and spa treatments. Chur's Freibad Sand outdoor pool is open in summer; the indoor Hallenbad Obere Au has slides, kiddie pools and daycare.

This region offers all ranges of hotels, from boutique and elegant in Chur, to historical inns, B&Bs and "sleep barrels" in the Bündner Herrschaft. The latter are what they sound like: large wine barrels repurposed to fit a bed for two, with a large window looking onto the valley below. Diogenes never had it so good. If you want a little more room in your room, try the wellness hotels in Bad Ragaz.

ZIEGELBRÜCKE–
RAPPERSWIL

Canal to lake, with fields and storks along the way

GLARUS,
ST. GALLEN

SIGHTS Linth Canal, Lake Zurich, Rapperswil old town

FOOD cafés, restaurants, fire pit, picnic areas

SPECIALTIES lake fish, Elmer Citro lemon soft drink, Linth corn chips, honey, almond croissants, *St.Galler Biber* (honey-sweetened cake filled with almond paste)

SWIMMING Linth Canal, Lake Zurich

HOTELS small historical hotels and B&Bs in Weesen and Rapperswil

 START
Ziegelbrücke

 FINISH
Rapperswil

DISTANCE
27.04 km

ELEVATION GAIN
-17 m

ASCENT
121 m

DESCENT
138 m

KID–FRIENDLY
yes

TOURISM
rapperswil-zuerichsee.ch

GPX TRACK
Flat Switzerland 2

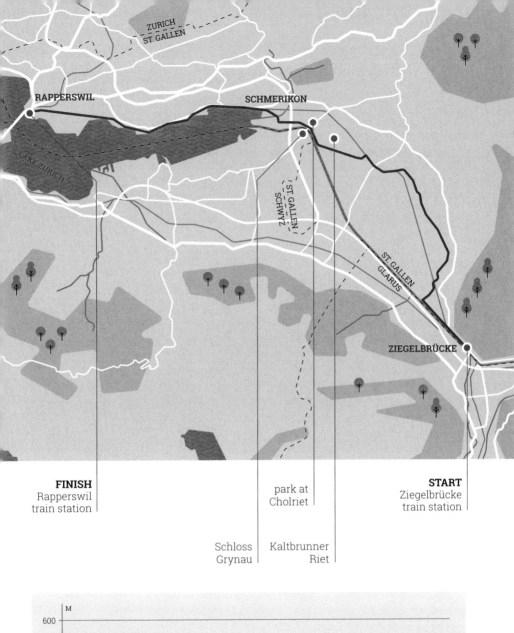

FINISH
Rapperswil
train station

park at
Cholriet

START
Ziegelbrücke
train station

Schloss
Grynau

Kaltbrunner
Riet

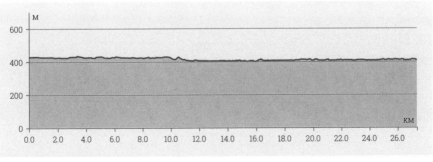

Route description

One of the more leisurely rides in this guide takes you along the Linth Canal from Ziegelbrücke to the top of Lake Zurich at Schmerikon, and from there beside the lake to Rapperswil. Follow national cycling route #9 to kilometer 11.6, then turn left off Uznacherstrasse onto the paved rural road that heads diagonally towards the Linth Canal. This takes you to Grynaustrasse and the Cholriet park across from Grynau Castle.

Cross Grynaustrasse and join route #9 again on Allmeinstrasse; follow it to Schmerikon and Rapperswil.

Schmerikon

Along the way

If you're doing this route in summer, you'll notice people bobbing down the Linth Canal on inflatables. If this floats your boat (sorry), you can do the bike tour backwards, renting bikes from SBB with pickup in Rapperswil and drop-off in Ziegelbrücke. Once there, get the boat you hired ahead of time and drift downstream to Schmerikon, where you'll give it back to the rental company and take the train home. Start early: this version of the tour will take all day. Spills are pretty much inevitable, so bring a floating waterproof bag for your valuables, unless you're looking for an excuse to buy a new smartphone.

Boat rental companies in Ziegelbrücke have come and gone over the years, but as this gets more popular, the offering has become more stable (search keywords: "Linth Boot").

Covered bridge over the Aa

Fans of storks may find joy in the marshlands of Kaltbrunner Riet outside of Benken – especially when the nearby hayfields have just been cut and the birds stalk through the cuttings, feasting on the insects and small wildlife uncovered by the farmers' harvesters.

The first half of the bike route is mostly out in the countryside, so bring your own picnic if you tend to get hungry at the start. There is a public playground with two grated fire pits outside Schänis (kilometer 4), with three tables, many benches, a covered hut and garbage cans.

Across from Cholriet park (kilometer 14.4), Schloss Grynau – a 13th century fortress built to keep an eye on river crossings – is unfortunately closed to visitors due to its rundown interior, but there is a restaurant across the street that serves good trout to make up for it.

Which means that food made by other people starts at Grynau, continuing along the lake from Schmerikon to Rapperswil. Lake fish is a specialty. As the biggest town on the route, Rapperswil naturally has a wider range of restaurants, and is a traditional lakeside spot for gorging on large, ice cream-based desserts.

Souvenir shopping is pretty much limited to Rapperswil, which as a local and international tourist destination has many boutiques and gift shops. Pop into a local bakery or cheese shop anywhere along the route for food specialties like alp cheeses, honey, Linth corn chips, almond croissants or a St.Galler Biber – a honey-sweetened cake filled with almond paste. Wash them down with an Elmer Citro – a lemon-flavored soft drink once the favorite of kids all over the region until colas took over.

Rapperswil

There are lots of public swimming spots along the Linth Canal and Lake Zurich. The park at Cholriet (kilometer 14.4) includes access to the canal, as well as benches and green spaces to spread a picnic blanket on. In summer there is often an ice cream truck set up in the parking lot. Schmerikon has a small beach across from the train station.

Overnighting at the start involves cycling 3 km east from Ziegelbrücke to Weesen on the west end of the Walensee, because the train no longer reaches that far. It's worth the quick trip though, because the village has the charm and relaxed lakeside atmosphere this guide is all about. At the other end, Rapperswil offers modernized historical accommodations in its old town. Otherwise this is a good one-day outing if you live a comfortable train ride away.

BRUGG–AARAU

Romans, castles, riverside woods and pools

AARGAU

SIGHTS

Vindonissa,
Königsfelden monastery,
Habsburg Castle,
Schinznach Bad

FOOD

cafés, restaurants,
fire pit, picnic areas

SPECIALTIES

Rüeblitorte (carrot cake),
Rüeblisuppe (carrot soup),
Chriesitötsch & Chriesiprägel
(cherry desserts), Café Papillon
(Brugg) & Brändli Bomben (Aarau)
chocolate pralines, Bachfisch
cookies (Aarau)

SWIMMING

Aare River, Halle & Freibad Brugg,
Aquarena Schinznach Bad,
Biobad Biberstein,
Badi Rupperswil-Auenstein,
Freibad Aarebrücke

HOTELS

mid-range, business
hotels & boutiques
in Aarau & Brugg

 START
Brugg

 FINISH
Aarau

 DISTANCE
23.89 km

 ELEVATION GAIN
32 m

 ASCENT
127 m

 DESCENT
95 m

 KID-FRIENDLY
yes

 **TOURISM**
aargautourismus.ch

 GPX TRACK
Flat Switzerland 3

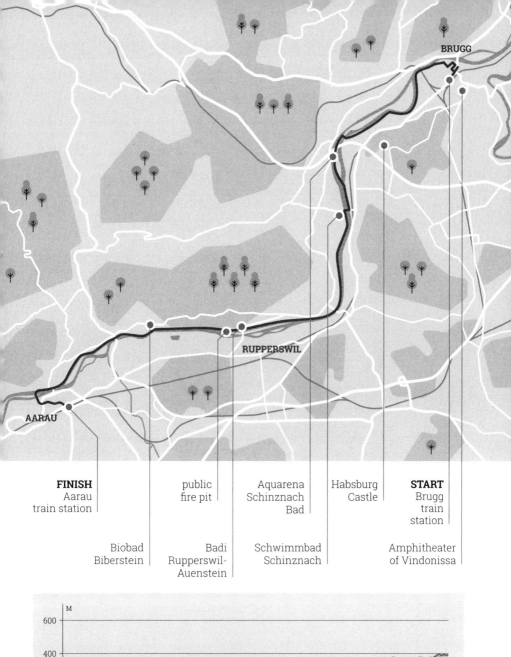

BRUGG

RUPPERSWIL

AARAU

FINISH
Aarau
train station

public
fire pit

Aquarena
Schinznach
Bad

Habsburg
Castle

START
Brugg
train
station

Biobad
Biberstein

Badi
Rupperswil-
Auenstein

Schwimmbad
Schinznach

Amphitheater
of Vindonissa

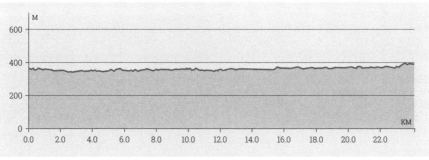

Route description

Bring your swimsuit. With five close swimming pools and countless riverside bathing spots along the way, you'll have lots of options for paddling around. And thanks to a trail meandering through the woods (well-provided with picnic spots), it's a cool option for summer heat. Fans of Romans and medieval castles might want to add a side trip to local hills.

Vindonissa

Another no-brainer in terms of finding your way, this excursion follows national cycling route #5/8. Turn right on Brugg's Bahnhofplatz and let the red bike signs be your guide. The route goes along the river all the way to Aarau, where you'll turn left just after the Kraftwerk Aarau power station (kilometer 22.6) onto route #3, which takes you up the slope to Aarau's old town and the train station.

Wallbach trail

With no worries about where you're going, you can save your energy for enjoying the water, trees, birds – and the odd industrial site. Mainly though, you'll have a quiet, relaxing ride through some of the Aare's nicest riverside woods, interspersed with benches for resting, and frequent access to the river for swimming. So right: bring your bathing suit.

Along the way

Just a few minutes behind the Brugg train station and only slightly uphill is the 1st century outdoor Roman amphitheater of Vindonissa and the Königsfelden monastery (just 200 m northeast at Königsfelderstr. 265), which was founded by the Habsburgs in 1308. If you want to know more about this dynasty of over-ambitious kings and empresses, follow the adjoining Hauserstrasse south to Habsburgstrasse, which will take you up the hill to what's left of the thousand-year Habsburg Castle, their founding seat.

While much of the original Habsburg fortress is in ruins, the restaurant in the remaining western section uses them as space for outdoor tables overlooking the scenic farmlands below. To get back to the Aare River, continue south down Schlossgasse/Dorfstrasse/Maienweg/ Habsburgstrasse and turn right towards Schinznach Bad on Kantonsstrasse/ Scherzerstrasse to Aarauerstrasse (turn left) to Aarestrasse (turn right), where you'll meet up with national cycling route #5/8 again on the river.

Aare

Brugg & Aarau have all the usual supermarkets for stocking up on picnic supplies. Most public pools come with the typical Swiss cafeteria also found in ski resorts, specializing in sausages, schnitzel, salad and the odd veggie offering. Even if they won't admit it, almost everyone is here for the French fries. There are plenty of cafés and restaurants in the villages along the way. As the largest towns, Brugg and Aarau have the most variety of cuisine.

There is a grated public fire pit just past the Kraftwerk Rupperswil-Auenstein power station. It has a large lawn with shade trees, benches and access to the river.

As in many parts of the country, the local specialties are food-based. The carrot cake (*Rüeblitorte*), carrot soup (*Rüeblisuppe*), cherries with cream of wheat (*Chriesitötsch*) and cherries cooked in apple sauce on bread with ice cream (*Chriesiprägel*), hint at former agricultural focal points.

The two main towns each make their own proud
confectioner's souvenir: chocolate pralines from Café Papillon
(Brugg); Brändli Bomben from Confiserie Brändli and the
flour-and-almond Bachfisch cookies from local shops (Aarau).

The thermal baths of Schinznach Bad include a waterpark.
Turn left at the footpath at kilometer 8.1. It meets up
with Badstrasse after about 300 m. You'll see a large
rehabilitation clinic at the north end of the road, which
circles around to the baths behind it. Other public pools
include Halle & Freibad Brugg, Biobad Biberstein, Badi
Rupperswil-Auenstein and Schwimmbad Schinznach.
Again: don't forget your bathing suit.

Accommodation for stops at either end of the route are in
the mid-range, with business hotels and boutiques in Aarau
and Brugg.

AARAU–OLTEN

Up a lazy river: picnics and old towns

AARAU,
SOLOTHURN

Old town Aarau,
Aare River,
Olten old town

cafés, restaurants,
fire pit, picnic areas

cookie and chocolate outlet stores

Aare River, Schwimmbad
Schachen/Aarau,
Badi Schönenwerd or
Schwimmbad Olten

mid-range, business hotels and
stylish boutiques in both Aarau
and Olten

 START
Aarau

 FINISH
Olten

 DISTANCE
15.84 km

 ELEVATION GAIN
13 m

 ASCENT
105 m

 DESCENT
92 m

 KID-FRIENDLY
yes

 **TOURISM**
oltentourismus.ch
aargautourismus.ch

 GPX TRACK
Flat Switzerland 4

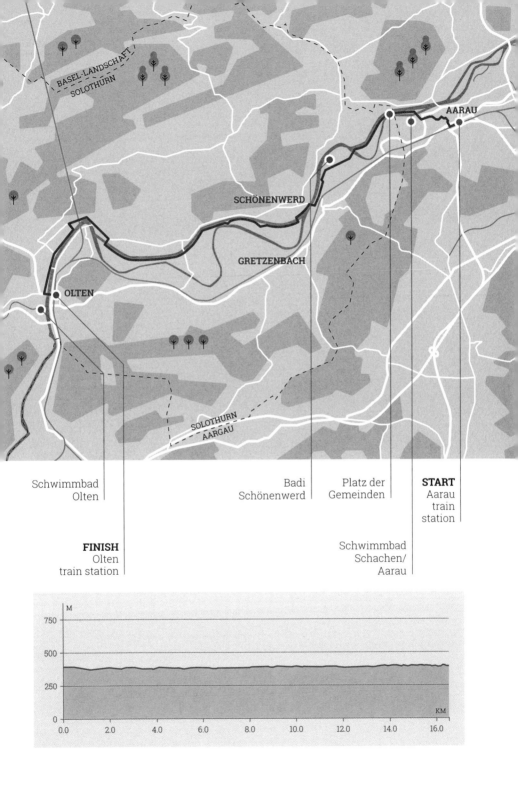

Schwimmbad
Olten

FINISH
Olten
train station

Badi
Schönenwerd

Platz der
Gemeinden

START
Aarau
train
station

Schwimmbad
Schachen/
Aarau

BASEL-LANDSCHAFT
SOLOTHURN

AARAU

SCHÖNENWERD

GRETZENBACH

OLTEN

SOLOTHURN
AARGAU

M

750

500

250

0

0.0   2.0   4.0   6.0   8.0   10.0   12.0   14.0   16.0

KM

Route description

Switzerland's second longest river (after the Rhine) is emerald blue in summer, moving through some of its lushest green countryside at a slow but steady pace. Let yourself be inspired by its tempo; the short distance gives you plenty of time to take in the sights.

Mostly you will cycle past parks, through woods, between farmer's fields – with the Aare beside you carrying water from the Bernese Alps to the North Sea.

There are only a few hundred meters or so that share a main thoroughfare; the rest of the way you'll be riding on local residential side streets or roads that are either dirt or paved and closed to anything but farming vehicles, hikers and bicycles.

Winznau

Schönenwerd

From the train station, following the red signs of national cycling route #8 will get you out Aarau's back door and down the hill to the Aare – after that it's pretty much just a matter of letting the river guide you all the way to Olten.

Look out for the small Giessenstrasse bridge (kilometer 13) to cross the Aare before you hit Olten's large railway shunting yard. Or miss it on purpose and see what's involved in moving around and maintaining most of northern Switzerland's rolling stock (see below).

Hungerberg

Along the way

Stroll, pedal, stroll along the easiest and shortest route in this guide. On either end, Aarau's 16th century old town and Olten's more compact one (with a nicely preserved covered bridge) are perfect for exploring.

Fans of all things railroad might be interested in the shunting yards east of Olten's train station. Instead of crossing the Giessenstrasse bridge (kilometer 13), continue along to the covered power station bridge, turn right on Haslistrasse, then left on Industriestrasse. The compound includes huge maintenance works for railway cars and engines, as well as the main railway control center for the Swiss Midlands. Tours in English are on request, see sbb.ch for details.

Both towns have more than their share of cafés and restaurants to hang in. For local color in Aarau, try the *Rüeblisuppe* (carrot soup), *Adrio* (a Swiss cousin of haggis, stuffed with pork), *Aargauerbraten* (pork roast stewed with dried plums), *Rüeblitorte* (carrot cake), *Chriesitötsch* or *Chriesiprägel* (cherry desserts). Olten's culinary claim to fame is the dissemination of the now quintessentially Swiss cervelat sausage. For many decades a staple of the restaurant at the train station – which was the major hub of Switzerland's railway system, with many travelers from all over the country holding meetings at this central point – it supposedly became so popular that its consumption rapidly spread throughout the rest of the land.

For lovers of outdoor grilling or their own perfect homemade sandwich, there are lots of spontaneous picnic spots along the way, as well as the official Platz der Gemeinden fire pit 2 km outside Aarau. There are lots of benches to sit on.

Erlinsbach

In Olten, dueling confectionaries will warm the heart of your inner or literal child: Lindt & Sprüngli has a chocolate outlet on the edge of the railyard and the Hug/Wernli cookie factory in the suburb of Trimbach serves its creations up in bulk.

Jump into the Aare on a hot day, or swim and lounge at Schwimmbad Schachen/Aarau, Badi Schönenwerd or Schwimmbad Olten.

While the accommodations in this region tend towards serviceable business hotels, stylish boutiques have arrived in both Aarau and Olten for those looking for a small-town getaway. Don't worry about hotels along the way: with a trail this pleasant you'll have no trouble reaching your destination.

OLTEN–SOLOTHURN

The flowery flatlands

SOLOTHURN,
BERN

SIGHTS

Olten old town, Solothurn old town and cathedral, Schloss Waldegg in Feldbrunnen-St. Niklaus

 START
Olten

FOOD

cafés, restaurants, picnic benches

 FINISH
Solothurn

 DISTANCE
38.91 km

SPECIALTIES

Buttenmost (rose hip paste), *Solothurner Torte*, *Funggi* (mashed potatoes and apples), *Biiremüsli* (dried pears fried in batter), (See Flat Switzerland 4 for more on Olten, Flat Switzerland 6 for more on Solothurn)

 ELEVATION GAIN
40 m

 ASCENT
269 m

 DESCENT
229 m

SWIMMING

Schwimmbad Olten, Freibad Solothurn

 KID-FRIENDLY
over 12, due to distance

 TOURISM
solothurn-city.ch
oltentourismus.ch

HOTELS

mid-range, business hotels, historical inns and stylish boutiques in Olten and Solothurn

 GPX TRACK
Flat Switzerland 5

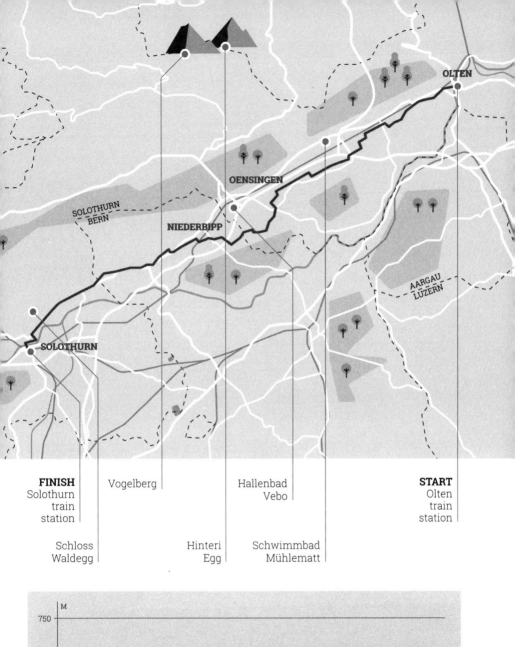

FINISH
Solothurn
train
station

Vogelberg

Hallenbad
Vebo

START
Olten
train
station

Schloss
Waldegg

Hinteri
Egg

Schwimmbad
Mühlematt

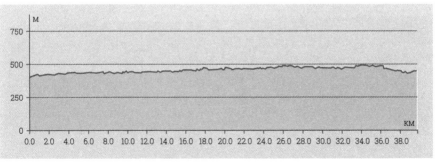

Route description

If you can't get enough of fields and country villages, this is your ride. It's a wonderful way to experience the flatlands of towns like the wonderfully named Niederbipp, where local organic farmers grow herbs such as lavender, peppermint, rose balm, lemon balm and clary sage for the ever-growing sustainable cosmetics industry. Bring a clear nose in spring and early summer, which is the best time to go – everything will be blooming, with canary yellow rapeseed fields out in full force.

Check wind conditions before you go; if there are headwinds, they can be strong.

Schlöpferhof

You'll mainly be following regional cycling route #50, with a detour at kilometer 31.5 outside Attiswil in Wibrunnen. From there, follow Solothurnstrasse to Flumenthal. Just after the Flumenthal train station, switch from the main road to the Schmittenweg cycling and pedestrian path on the south side, and back to the north side at the next crossroads (there are signs). You're now cycling along Baselstrasse, where you'll pick up #50 again at kilometer 37.9, just outside Solothurn's old town. Turn left down towards the Aare River and follow it to the Solothurn train station.

Kestenholz
©Bee Bonnet

Along the way

Olten's well-preserved medieval old town is very concentrated and stuffed with cafes and restaurants. For the full effect, use the covered wooden bridge southwest of the train station to cross the Aare. Thanks to 17th & 18th century patricians, Solothurn's center is architecturally rich in baroque townhouses and an impressive neoclassical cathedral. If you have time along the way, Schloss Waldegg in Feldbrunnen-St. Niklaus (kilometer 36.8) features an awe-inspiring driveway up to the castle past lush lawns and a beautiful garden. Inside, the permanent collection shows you how the local 1% and ambassadors to France made do while living in the region.

This is bench-picnic country, as most of the private fields are being used to feed animals or farm your future meals. Luckily you're in Switzerland, where benches along trails every few 100 meters are pretty much mandatory. Olten and Solothurn have a wide range of restaurants and cuisines, and most villages have at least a vending machine for snacks at train stations, if not a town local for food and drink.

Keep an eye open for farm shops, which sell their own produce, milk, juice or eggs. Olten, Solothurn, larger towns like Oensingen and some villages have gift shops with local crafts, as well as bakeries with yummy specialties.

Unless you want to just stick your feet into a local creek or make a detour to the much smaller local pools in Egerkingen (Schwimmbad Mühlematt outdoor) or Oensingen (Hallenbad Vebo indoor), there's no real swimming during this route. But at either end, Olten and Solothurn's *Badis* more than make up for that fact. Both feature large outdoor pools and direct access to the Aare, as well as lawns, beach volleyball courts, slides, kiddie pools, playgrounds and cafeterias.

Solothurn

Schwimmbad Olten has a lengths pool, a diving pool and a play pool with intricate slides around a "castle". Directly across the river there are public steps down to the Aare for more spontaneous swimming. Freibad Solothurn is even larger, with three outdoor pools and shade for the children's area.

For overnights, there are business hotels, historical inns and stylish boutiques in Olten and Solothurn, with simpler hotels in the villages in between.

SOLOTHURN–BIEL

Along the Aare to the foot of the Jura

SOLOTHURN,
BERN

SIGHTS

Solothurn old town and cathedral, Altreu, Biel's old town, Cité du Temps watch museum in Biel

 START

Solothurn

 FINISH

Biel

FOOD

cafés, restaurants, fire pit, picnic areas

 DISTANCE

31.79 km

 ELEVATION GAIN

2 m

SPECIALTIES

walnut oil, *Buttenmost* (rose hip paste), Solothurner torte (Solothurn, see Flat Switzerland 5 for more), watches, wine, *Tête de Moine, Damassine* and absinthe, lake fish (perch, pike, pollan) (Biel)

 ASCENT

97 m

 DESCENT

95 m

SWIMMING

Aare, Solothurn Badi, Strandbad Biel, Strandboden Biel

 KID-FRIENDLY

yes, over 12

 TOURISM

solothurn-city.ch
j3l.ch

HOTELS

mid-range, business hotels, historical inns and stylish boutiques in Biel and Solothurn

 GPX TRACK

Flat Switzerland 6

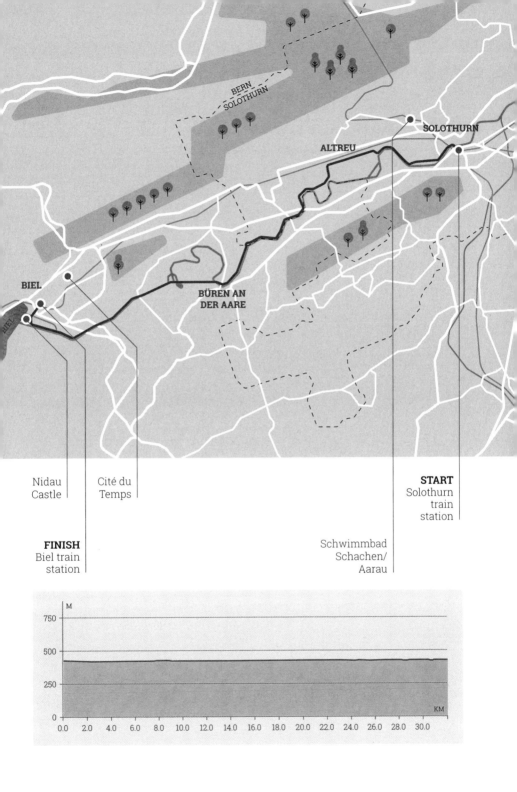

BERN
SOLOTHURN

SOLOTHURN

ALTREU

BIEL

BÜREN AN
DER AARE

Nidau
Castle

Cité du
Temps

START
Solothurn
train
station

FINISH
Biel train
station

Schwimmbad
Schachen/
Aarau

Route description

Pedal around Solothurn's beautiful old town, have a coffee or cold drink at one of its riverside cafés. Then it's off through kilometers of rapeseed, wheat and corn fields to the green villages of the Aare – Altreu, Staad and Büren an der Aare – arriving at the northeastern tip of Lake Biel. Splash in the lake and go for a stroll through Biel's old town.

From Solothurn, follow national cycling route #5/8 from Solothurn to Biel. Got it? Good. The pure simplicity of this tour in terms of directions means we have more room to look at all the things you can do while you're there.

Gluztenhof, looking onto Solothurner's "Witi"

Along the way

Solothurn's period under the rule (thumb?) of local patricians from the 17th and 18th centuries left an architectural mark, with 18 buildings currently listed as Swiss heritage sites. The most opulent of these is arguably the imposing neoclassical St. Ursus Cathedral, which to first-timers looks somewhat overly grand for Solothurn's relatively small old town. Its main features date to 1773 and the interior is considered subdued for rococo (if there is such a thing). But as we know, size doesn't matter: Solothurn's center is definitely worth a visit, with picturesque spots like the market square, an astounding clock tower and the massive medieval Basel Gate.

The first village west of Solothurn, Altreu, is famous for its storks. Every March, they arrive to build (or re-build) their nests on top of many of the old houses in the village, staying there until early August, when their offspring are ready to fly away on their own. Bring a zoom lens.

A listed heritage site, the village of Büren an der Aare is a Sunday afternoon destination for locals, thanks to its covered bridge and a veritable plethora of restaurants. It also has many gift shops offering local handicrafts.

Nidau Castle is of interest to amateur and professional hydro engineers. Just on the border of Biel at kilometer 31.7, it has a permanent exhibition of the historical "Jura Water Correction" of the 19th and 20th centuries, which kept devastating floods from regularly damaging the Three-Lakes Region between La Sarraz in the south and Luterbach east of Solothurn. In addition to diverting the Aare River into Lake Biel, the region's engineers built a series of canals to keep water levels regular all year round.

Büren an der Aare

Biel's gorgeous medieval old town is full of charm and restaurants. Plan around a market day when you go for local color and spontaneous shopping.

Fans of architecture will love the Swatch Group's Cité du Temps watch museum in Biel. Even if you don't go inside, the building is worth gawping at from the southwest entrance: it looks like an enormous snake swallowed an even bigger hippopotamus. Take the bicycle path upstream from the lake along the Schüss River. The museum is at about kilometer 4; it's hard to miss.

Cité du Temps Museum, Biel

As far as souvenirs go, you're traveling from the land of cervelat and beer to that of fish, wine and the spirits of the nearby Jura region. Which is not to say Biel has no sausages: specialties like the *saucisson vaudois* have long since come up from the south. Also look for walnut oil, *Buttenmost* (rose hip paste), Solothurner Torte in Solothurn, and watches, wine, *Damassine* and absinthe, lake fish (perch, pike, pollan) in Biel. Check local cheese shops for regional varieties like Tête de Moine.

Swimming along the Aare is mostly unorganized, with parks few and far between – so find a spot, jump in, watch out for boats, scramble back out. Otherwise, public pools with river or lake access nicely measure up to Switzerland's high standards. The Solothurn Badi has three pools, slides and all the amenities. Strandbad Biel is a fee-based public beach on Lake Biel. A few hundred meters west the free lawns of Strandboden park are spacious, with rowboats and pedalos for rent.

Both Biel and Solothurn have a variety of business hotels, historical inns and stylish boutiques.

BIEL–NEUCHÂTEL

Villas and vineyards along quiet lakes

BERN,
NEUCHÂTEL

SIGHTS

villas and vineyards,
Biel & Neuchâtel old towns,
Cité du Temps watch
museum in Biel

FOOD

cafés, restaurants,
fire pit, picnic areas

SPECIALTIES

wine, watches, *Tête de Moine*,
Damassine and absinthe,
lake fish (perch, pike, pollan)

SWIMMING

Strandbad and Strandboden Biel;
small parks in Twann, Ligerz
and La Neuveville; Piscine du
Landeron in Le Landeron;
Plage du Vieux Port in Hauterive

HOTELS

mid-range, business hotels,
historical inns and stylish
boutiques in Biel and Neuchâtel

 START
Biel

 FINISH
Neuchâtel

 DISTANCE
34.30 km

 **ELEVATION
GAIN**
1 m

 ASCENT
219 m

 DESCENT
218 m

 **KID-
FRIENDLY**
yes, over 12

 TOURISM
j3l.ch

 GPX TRACK
Flat Switzerland 7

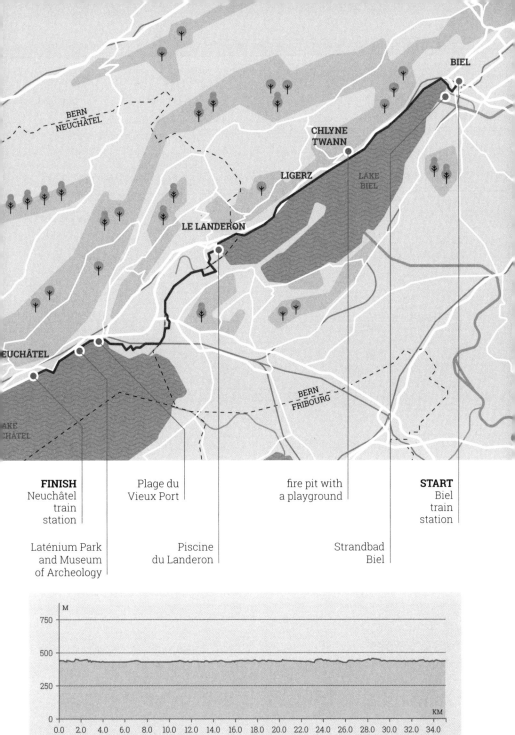

BIEL

BERN
NEUCHÂTEL

CHLYNE
TWANN

LIGERZ

LAKE
BIEL

LE LANDERON

NEUCHÂTEL

BERN
FRIBOURG

LAKE
CHÂTEL

FINISH	Plage du	fire pit with	**START**
Neuchâtel	Vieux Port	a playground	Biel
train			train
station			station

Laténium Park	Piscine	Strandbad
and Museum	du Landeron	Biel
of Archeology		

Route description

This route sticks to the lakeshore, meaning you can stop and watch the sparkling blue water from a bench anytime. While you're sitting there, turn around for a view of the vineyards along the lake's slopes. Or slow down past villas with their own waterfront lawns and docks – and dream about spending an entire summer here.

Biel, lakeside

A 12-km stretch on and off the main road makes this route less suitable for small children: traffic can be quite heavy and even though there are dedicated crossings and turn-offs, they can be tricky. There are options for getting off your bike and walking along sidewalks or pedestrian paths. Please use your own judgement.

Leave the Biel train station through its southern exit onto Robert-Walser-Platz which leads to Aarbergstrasse. Cross it and the little Zihl River, continue along Dr.-Schneider-Strasse. When you hit kilometer .5, turn right into the park and past the public pool. After another 200 m, cross the river again where it flows into the lake. Keep going (you'll cross two small canals) to the end of the park at Neuenburgstrasse.

Cross Neuenburgstrasse, turn left and go south for 1.6 km to the Schlössli off-ramp (kilometer 3.3). Go down to the lakeside lane called Im Rusel; at kilometer 4 its name changes to Strandweg. This lakeside lane is open only to local vehicles, bicycles and pedestrians. Follow it to the pedestrian zone just before Ligerz (kilometer 10.5). Either turn right up to the main street (traffic is somewhat calmer here thanks to the 50 km/h speed limit) or get off and stroll with your bike for 1.5 km to where bicycles are again allowed to join the lane (if you've taken the main road, there is a sign at kilometer 12 pointing you back down to the lake).

Ligerz

The lakeside lane changes names seven times on the map as it goes in and out of towns, but it's always the same path. In La Neuveville turn left at kilometer 16.1 onto Bellerive, which takes you to the end of the lake and Le Landeron.

At kilometer 17.4 turn left onto Route de la Piscine, which turns into Rue du Lac. Follow that to kilometer 18.2 and turn left onto Rue Saint-Maurice into Le Landeron's tiny old town. At the other end, take the main road for 100 m and turn left onto Rue de Berne. From there continue over the Thielle Canal, and turn right on the other side at Grissachmoos. You're now on regional cycling route #50, which you can follow all the way to Neuchâtel.

In Neuchâtel itself, you can either continue on route #50 up the steep hill to the train station, or at 35 km turn right onto Rue Coulon to Avenue du Premier-Mars, cross that and take the Fun'Ambule funicular up. Bicycles need their own ticket and are only allowed if there is space available, so avoid rush hour.

Along the way

The vintner towns of Twann, Ligerz and La Neuveville offer the full local wine-and-dine experience. If your focus is more on the outdoors, there are many benches along the lane and in town parks where you can enjoy your picnic lunch, as well as a fire pit with a playground at Chlyne Twann (kilometer 9.7).

History buffs are encouraged to stop off at the Laténium at kilometer 31.4. This archeological museum houses hundreds of thousands of objects from local digs, covering an uninterrupted period from the Middle Paleolithic age through the Romans to today.

If you've had a dusty train ride to Biel, make your first pit stop at the lake down the street from the train station. Choose between the full amenities of the Strandbad Biel public beach, or the free lawns of Strandboden park on the west side. Small parks dot the lake in Twann, Ligerz and La Neuveville. The Piscine du Landeron in Le Landeron has both lake swimming and a large public pool; the free Plage du Vieux Port park in Hauterive on Lake Neuchâtel has a number of man-made bays that keep the water warmer.

In addition to the wines of Lake Biel, specialties are colored by the adjoining Jura region, so local terroir shops carry Tête de Moine cheese and various spirits like *Damassine* and absinthe.

For overnights, you'll find business hotels and stylish boutiques in Biel and Neuchâtel, and small historical inns along the whole route.

Wingreis

NEUCHÂTEL–YVERDON-LES-BAINS

Swimming from castles to vineyards

NEUCHÂTEL, VAUD

SIGHTS

Neuchâtel, vineyards below Bevaix, lakeside village of Petit Cortaillod, vineyards of St-Aubin-Sauges and Vaumarcus, Yverdon-les-Bains

FOOD

cafés, restaurants, fire pit, picnic areas

SPECIALTIES

absinthe, *eau-de-vie de prunes* (plum schnaps), *jambon cuit dans l'asphalte* (ham cooked in asphalt), *flûtes* (twisted savory puff pastry sticks), *sèche* (flatbread topped with bacon or caraway seeds), Sugus candies

SWIMMING

Plage Suchard, Plage Petit-Cortaillod, Plage de la Pointe-du-Grain, Plage du port Concise, Grandson swimming park, Plage d'Yverdon-les-Bains

HOTELS

business & historical hotels and stylish boutiques in Neuchâtel; business & mid-range hotels, camping and a premium spa in Yverdon

 START
Neuchâtel

 FINISH
Yverdon-les-Bains

 DISTANCE
41.92 km

 ELEVATION GAIN
0 m

 ASCENT
381 m

 DESCENT
381 m

 KID-FRIENDLY
yes, 12 and up due to distance

 TOURISM
j3l.ch

 GPX TRACK
Flat Switzerland 8

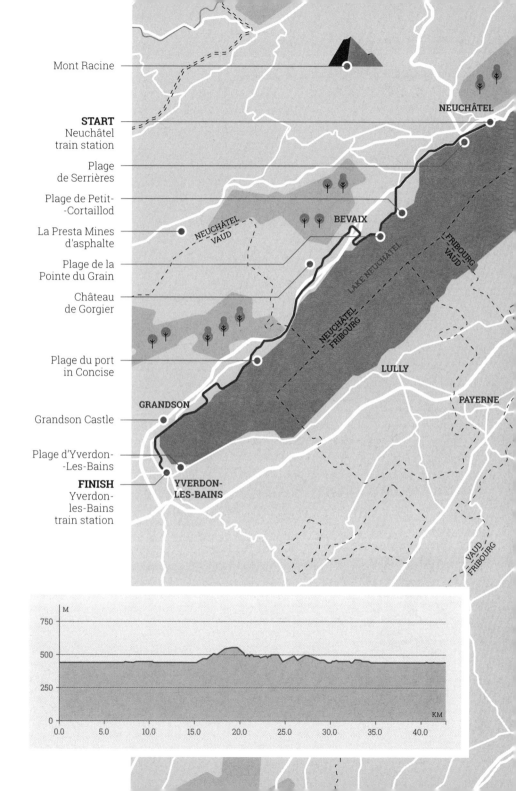

Mont Racine

START
Neuchâtel
train station

Plage
de Serrières

Plage de Petit-
-Cortaillod

La Presta Mines
d'asphalte

Plage de la
Pointe du Grain

Château
de Gorgier

Plage du port
in Concise

Grandson Castle

Plage d'Yverdon-
-Les-Bains

FINISH
Yverdon-
les-Bains
train station

NEUCHÂTEL

NEUCHÂTEL
VAUD

BEVAIX

FRIBOURG
VAUD

LAKE NEUCHÂTEL

NEUCHÂTEL
FRIBOURG

LULLY

PAYERNE

GRANDSON

YVERDON-
LES-BAINS

VAUD
FRIBOURG

M

750

500

250

0

0.0   5.0   10.0   15.0   20.0   25.0   30.0   35.0   40.0   KM

Route description

An easy, quiet cycle through Switzerland's "Wild West" of vineyards, castles and beaches of all sizes. With lots of opportunities to swim, stop for a picnic or hang in a lakeside café or restaurant.

This is another easy route in terms of directions: all you have to do is follow regional cycling Route #50 from Neuchâtel to Yverdon-les-Bains.

Most of the way is as flat as this book promises, with one ascent to make things vertically interesting. Starting at kilometer 13.5 on Bevaix's lakeshore, the route travels up 112 meters to kilometer 19.1, where you will be rewarded by a view over Lake Neuchâtel to the Alps in the distance.

But as you're zipping down the hill from there, be careful at kilometer 19.6 – the driveway of the Château de Gorgier is so inviting that you may just let yourself glide up it. Which is what I did when I rode this route a few years back, thinking it would be nice to check out for a future castle tour. I was promptly welcomed by two guard dogs and man who pointed out the very small "Private Property" sign to the right of the open front gates.

Neither should you let yourself be tempted at kilometer 14.9 by the path that seems to continue on along the lake. It does, but it's a hiking trail that gets continuously narrower and after about 2 km you'll end up having to schlepp your bicycle up a very steep path to get to the nearest main road – or turn around and go back the way you came. Instead, keep following Route #50 by turning right up the hill.

Colombier

Along the way

Put time aside to meander the narrow, cobblestone streets lined with medieval townhouses in the compact old towns of Neuchâtel and Yverdon, each with its own impressive castle. The gorgeous vineyards of this region continue onwards from Neuchâtel and are dotted with more castles, many of which – unfortunately for us – are privately owned. One exception is the medieval fortress in Grandson that looks like it's straight out of a fairy tale.

Food and drink will not be a challenge: there are of course plenty of cafés, restaurants and supermarkets on either end, and other places to eat are easy to find in the charming, leisurely little villages along the route.

A wonderful side-trip from Neuchâtel to La Presta Mines d'asphalte (about 30 minutes by train) is a must for the adventurous. About 50 meters from the La Presta Mines d'asphalte train stop, the Café des Mines cooks whole hams in melted asphalt (*jambon cuit dans l'asphalte*). This unusual method was invented almost 100 years ago by workers from the nearby mine and although operations there have long since ceased, this odd bit of traditional cuisine has continued. The former mine is also open for tours.

There are fire pits at the Plage d'Yverdon-Les-Bains at the southwest end of Lake Neuchâtel, with a woodpile and picnic tables. This large, free park also has a restaurant and snack bars.

A fun specialty to take home with you is Sugus. Initially a Swiss innovation dating back to 1931 from Swiss chocolatier Suchard SA, these chewy fruit candies are now owned by an international conglomerate and enjoyed around the globe – they have become a favorite in East Asian countries during the Lunar New Year.

Vaumarcus

You'll find the influence of the nearby Jura Mountains in the old towns of Neuchâtel and Yverdon. Both have nice delicatessens, where you'll find spirits like eau-de-vie de *prunes* and absinthe, which of course makes the heart grow warmer.

Many of the *plages* along Lake Neuchâtel are free (as are all on this list) and a few boast that rarity in Switzerland: a sandy beach. This includes the Plage des Jeunes-Rives and the well-appointed Plage d'Yverdon-les-Bains (see also Flat Switzerland 9 for more details). Expect pebbles at the Plage Suchard and Plage de Serrières in Neuchâtel and the Plage de Petit-Cortaillod. If you like things quiet, keep an eye open as you go and discover small pebble beaches like the Plage de la Pointe-du-Grain before Bevaix or the Plage du port in Concise.

Plage
de la Pointe-
-du-Grain

Overnights are easy to plan in this region, with business & historical hotels and stylish boutiques in Neuchâtel, historical hotels along the route, as well as business & mid-range hotels, camping and a premium spa in Yverdon.

YVERDON-LES-BAINS -LA SARRAZ

VAUD

The meditative calm of the flatlands

SIGHTS

Lake Neuchâtel, Yverdon old town, agricultural landscape, small-plane-spotting, La Sarraz Castle

FOOD

specialty shops, cafés, fire pits, restaurants in Yverdon; some in La Sarraz

SPECIALTIES

saucisson vaudois (pork sausage), fish, cheese, truffles (the in-ground kind), *amandine* (almond honey cake)

SWIMMING

Lake Neuchâtel, La Sarraz outdoor pool

HOTELS

business & mid-range hotels, camping and premium spa in Yverdon; economy hotel in La Sarraz

 START

Yverdon-les-Bains

 FINISH

La Sarraz

 DISTANCE

22.23 km

ELEVATION GAIN

63 m

ASCENT

130 m

DESCENT

67 m

 KID-FRIENDLY

yes

 TOURISM

yverdonlesbains region.ch

 GPX TRACK

Flat Switzerland 9

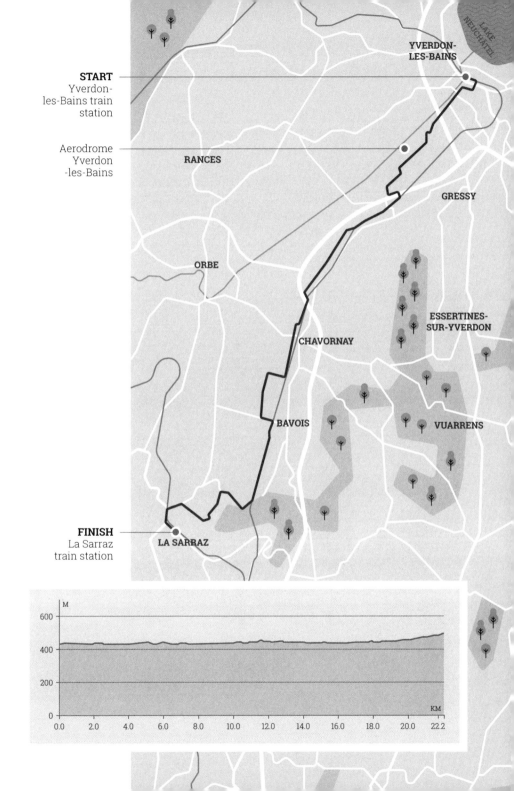

START
Yverdon-
les-Bains train
station

Aerodrome
Yverdon
-les-Bains

RANCES

**YVERDON-
LES-BAINS**

LAKE
NEUCHÂTEL

GRESSY

ORBE

CHAVORNAY

**ESSERTINES-
SUR-YVERDON**

BAVOIS

VUARRENS

FINISH
La Sarraz
train station

LA SARRAZ

M

600

400

200

0

KM

0.0   2.0   4.0   6.0   8.0   10.0   12.0   14.0   16.0   18.0   20.0   22.2

Route description

This one is good for kids, with hardly any traffic along the route, which is mostly along rural roads closed to vehicles except tractors and bicycles. But what it's really great for is a lone cycle away from the hectic world. When you want to just glide through flat serenity for a few hours. For the first few kilometers, a light-aircraft airport has a parallel runway doing a fair bit of business, so you can watch little planes softly go up and down as you pass along rows of poplars waving in the breeze. It's also short enough for a return trip, ending up at the beach back in Yverdon (see swimming details below).

Finding your way is easy: just follow national route #5 from the Yverdon-les-Bains train station to La Sarraz. That's it.

Chemin de la Grande Prairie

Place Pestalozzi in Yverdon-les-Bains

Along the way

Before you cycle away from Yverdon, take some time to peruse the old town and its beautiful mix of baroque and medieval architecture. Place Pestalozzi deserves special mention, flanked as it is by the town's 17th century Protestant church and town hall, its 13th century Yverdon Castle (in which educational reformer Johann Heinrich Pestalozzi founded a school) and a tasty array of cafés and restaurants.

Most of this bike route winds among the fields in the flatlands between its start and finish. So if you're not starting with lunch in one of the many restaurants in Yverdon, it's best to pack a picnic. Or better yet, do a shopping tour of the old town's specialty stores for wine, meat, cheese, veggies, bread and whatever else takes your fancy – like the local almond honey cake, whose built-in energy should keep you going for several days at least. After Yverdon, there are a few cafés and restaurants in the villages on the way to La Sarraz, which has a small number to choose from as well. These may be closed between 2pm and 7pm.

The gift shops in Yverdon and La Sarraz focus on artisanal local products – they are a great place to browse for special presents for yourself or anyone who wasn't able to make the trip with you.

Coming up on its 1,000th birthday, La Sarraz Castle is now a museum stuffed with – by its curators' count – about 13,000 furnishings, paintings and household objects acquired over the centuries by the generations of barons who presided over it. It's all displayed as if they still lived there, so you can pretend you do too. It has a large garden and a pleasant café, as well as a horse museum in the barn.

La Sarraz

If you like your swim to be a big part of the end of a cycling trip, you might want to do this route backwards or make it a return trip. Although La Sarraz has a nice outdoor pool with a restaurant, Yverdon boasts Lake Neuchâtel and a large beach-front park. A summer destination for locals and domestic tourists at the southwest end of the lake, its wide-ranging (and free) infrastructure includes fire pits, a sandy beach, a playground, lawns, shade trees, picnic tables, changing rooms, bathrooms and showers. There is also an adjoining campground and a restaurant.

If you're staying overnight in Yverdon, choose from business and mid-range accommodations, as well as a premium spa with thermal baths. La Sarraz has a few small economy hotels that do the job nicely.

LAUSANNE– MONTREUX

Gliding through lakeside wineries, villages and quays

VAUD

SIGHTS
Ouchy, Lutry, Cully, St-Saphorin, Vevey, vineyards

FOOD
cafés, restaurants (international cuisines), picnic areas

SPECIALTIES
wine, *boutefas* (pork sausage), *perche* (perch), *salée au sucre* (cream cake) See also Flat Switzerland 11

SWIMMING
Lake Geneva, especially from Louis Bourget Park to the Jetée-de-la-Compagnie in Lausanne, free *plages* in Lutry, Moratel, Rivaz, Crottaz, Vevey, La-Tour-de-Peilz. Fee-based in Lausanne Bellerive, Pully, Vevey-Corseaux

HOTELS
all ranges, especially luxury, premium and boutique. Camping in Moratel

START
Lausanne

FINISH
Montreux

DISTANCE
27.41 km

ELEVATION GAIN
-62 m

ASCENT
179 m

DESCENT
241 m

KID-FRIENDLY
no, due to main road traffic after Lutry

TOURISM
lausanne-tourisme.ch

montreuxriviera.com

GPX TRACK
Flat Switzerland 10

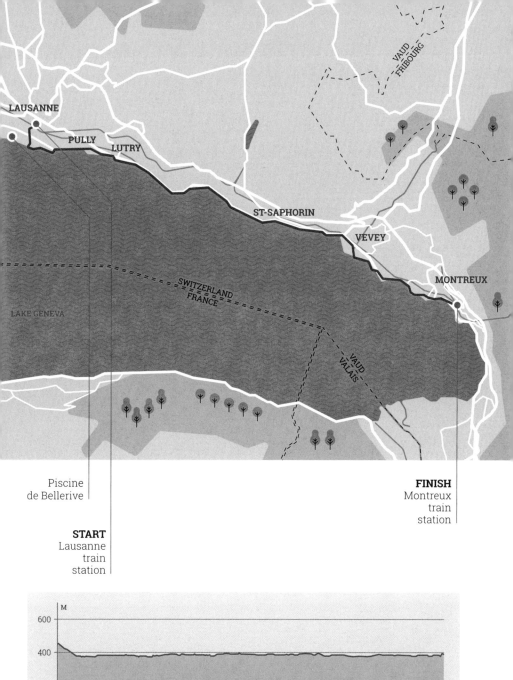

LAUSANNE

PULLY

LUTRY

ST-SAPHORIN

VEVEY

MONTREUX

VAUD
FRIBOURG

SWITZERLAND
FRANCE

VAUD
VALAIS

LAKE GENEVA

Piscine
de Bellerive

START
Lausanne
train
station

FINISH
Montreux
train
station

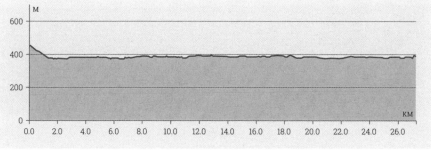

Route description

Stretch a 2-hour bike ride into a whole day by stopping at village *plages*, benches, cafés and restaurants to take in gorgeous Lake Geneva, the vineyards in the hills above you and the quays you're often cycling along. And if the main road has a lot of traffic on it, there's always a sidewalk to turn onto and admire the scenery.

From Lausanne's Place de la Gare, turn left down Avenue William-Fraisse, which turns into Avenue Frédéric-César-de-la-Harpe, and follow that all the way down to the lake.

Turn left on the Place de la Navigation, where you'll see the red SwitzerlandMobility cycling signs – follow route #1 to kilometer 7.2 at the roundabout just east of Lutry's old town. Leave route #1 there by turning right onto Route de Lavaux (kilometer 6.8), turn down towards the lake onto Route de Lausanne in Cully (kilometer 9.9), which will turn into Route de Vevey (kilometer 10.7) and rejoin Route de Lausanne again (kilometer 11.2). Continue along this main road all the way to Vevey and rejoin route #1 there by keeping right on the roundabout in front of the train station and turning right onto Avenue Paul-Cérésole (kilometer 20.3). Follow route #1 along Lake Geneva to Montreux, where you'll turn left onto Avenue des Alps (kilometer 26.7) and take it up to the train station.

Lutry

Along the way

The former harbor of Ouchy is now dominated by a lakeside quay with slips for sailboats and lake cruise ships. Bicycles are allowed on its Place de la Navigation, so feel free to noodle around the fountains to the carousel that's open year-round, weather permitting, and continue along the shore park for a first impression of what's to come: tree-lined paths dotted with cafés and restaurants, lined with benches, all offering views of the French Alps across the blue waters of Lake Geneva. Most of the lakeside villages on the route to Montreux have smaller versions of this, including Lutry, Cully and Vevey. My favorite is the old town of Lutry, whose shops and picturesque Quai Gustave-Doret just sigh "vacation."

Cully

Epesses

This is another route where you won't go hungry. All price ranges are covered, from lakeside snack bars, cafés and restaurants to supermarkets and specialty shops for picnic supplies. If you've brought your own lunch, every quay has an array of benches and parks are plentiful, so go ahead and bring a blanket to spread out.

The Lavaux Vineyard Terraces are famous mainly for their whites (Chasselas, but also Chardonnay and Sauvignon Blanc) with reds that are also worth a sip (Pinot Noir, Gamay, Merlot and the lesser-known but equally delicious Gamaret and Garanoir). You'll find plenty of wineries, bars and restaurants for tasting, purchasing and – depending on your mood – indulging in a glass or two. All wineries ship as well.

Bakeries are a wonderful place to get mouthwatering artisanal souvenirs from this region. Lutry has three excellent ones in its old town. From savory tarts (*ramequins*) filled with cheese, onions or bacon cubes and croissants injected with chocolate to homemade chocolate confections, you'll find something for everyone – especially yourself. Some bakeries will ship your purchases home to you, so you don't have to worry about chocolate dripping onto your tires as you cycle in the sun.

The swimming options are numerous. Lausanne has a 5-km expanse of leisure infrastructure that runs along the lake from Parc Louis-Bourget through to the Piscine de Bellerive and Jetée-de-la-Compagnie to the end of the Quai d'Ouchy at the Parc du Denantou. All of it offers lake access for free except the piscine, which charges admission for its showers, lockers, lawns, shade trees, four pools (bathing, wading, slide, lengths with diving boards), playground, beach volleyball court and large inflatables in the lake.

There are free, simple *plages* with lawns, shade trees and lake access in Lutry, Moratel, Rivaz, Crottaz, Vevey and La-Tour-de-Peilz. Fee-based ones with showers, lockers, lawns, shade trees, pools and lake access are located in Pully and Vevey-Corseaux. This is not an exhaustive list. If you suddenly need a swim, just keep an eye out – another *plage* is just around the bend. You can also jump in from anywhere along the quays, just watch for occasional *baignade interdite* (no swimming) signs and remember swimming is not allowed near boat jetties.

It's no surprise that world's first hotel management school is located in Lausanne: this region has whatever you need in terms of accommodations. You'll find everything from 19th century *grandes hôtels* and 21st century boutiques to affordable B&Bs and even campgrounds (in Vidy and Moratel), but the majority are in the luxury segment, so now's the time to splurge if you feel so inclined.

Dézaley

MONTREUX–AIGLE

Freddie, Byron and Lake Geneva

VAUD

SIGHTS Montreux, lakeside quay, Château de Chillon, Aigle

FOOD cafés, restaurants (international cuisines), fire pit, picnic areas

SPECIALTIES papet Vaudois (*saucisson Vaudois* with leeks and potatoes), *tarte au vin* (sweet pastry topped with white wine, cinnamon and butter). See also Flat Switzerland 10

SWIMMING Lake Geneva, Piscine du Casino Montreux, Piscine communale Les Marines, Villeneuve

HOTELS luxury, premium, boutique, mid-range, historical, camping

 START
Montreux

 FINISH
Aigle

 DISTANCE
16.63 km

 ELEVATION GAIN
17 m

 ASCENT
118 m

 DESCENT
101 m

 KID-FRIENDLY
yes, with caution at kilometer 8.3

 TOURISM
montreuxriviera.com
aigle-leysin-lesmosses.ch

 GPX TRACK
Flat Switzerland 11

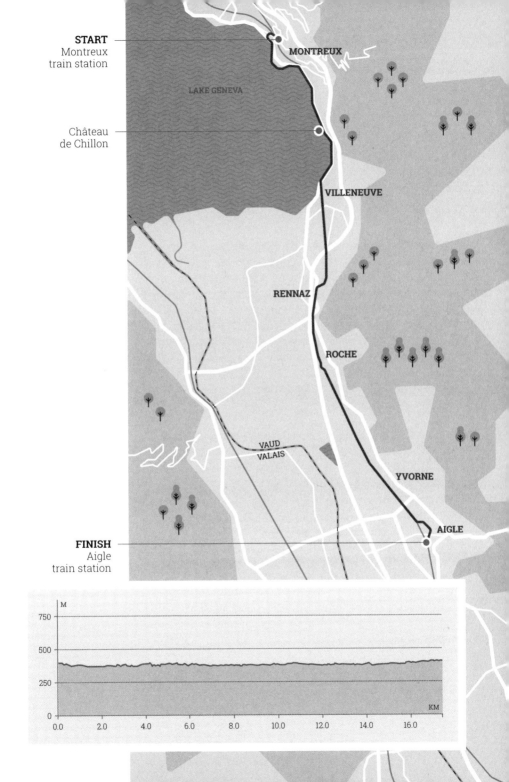

START
Montreux
train station

Château
de Chillon

MONTREUX

LAKE GENEVA

VILLENEUVE

RENNAZ

ROCHE

VAUD
VALAIS

YVORNE

AIGLE

FINISH
Aigle
train station

M

750

500

250

0

0.0   2.0   4.0   6.0   8.0   10.0   12.0   14.0   16.0   KM

Route description

This breathtaking ride is short for two good reasons. First, because you might want to stop at Château de Chillon for a few hours at the start and sit on an outdoor patio in Aigle to taste some wine at the end. Or perhaps combine Flat Switzerland 10 to 14 into a multiday cycling tour from Lausanne to Brig, which means there are longer segments to come.

It's the only section in this guide not to follow a national cycling route. At Montreux's train station, go northwest along Avenue des Alpes for 200 m to the roundabout and turn left down Rue de la Gare. At the bottom, turn left onto Grand Rue, which turns into Avenue Claude-Nobs, turn right down Rue Alexandre-Emery and turn left onto the quay (kilometer 0.55). Follow the quay all the way to the Route Cantonale in Villeneuve (kilometer 5.6) and cross there (it's safest to use the crosswalk) to Avenue Comtes de Savoie. (If you're with children, consider switching to national cycling route #1 at kilometer 5.6.)

Go past the train station, turn left onto Rue des Remparts and left again onto Route du Pont-Noir. At kilometer 8.3 there's a tricky bit: The path comes to the double roundabout at the busy Route du Simplon. Take the roundabout lane that crosses the route and once you're over, immediately turn left onto the path that runs parallel to Route du Simplon. You'll now be safely headed towards Aigle.

Keep this in mind if you are bringing kids; their level of cycling experience will be crucial. There are unfortunately no crosswalks as an alternative – even though the roundabout is directly in front of a police station.

Follow the lane to kilometer 9.1, where you will cross Route du Village onto the continuation of the lane, now called Chemin de la Rotta. Take it to the railway tracks and follow them to Aigle, where the lane will be called Chemin des Lieugex.

At kilometer 15.7 turn left onto Chemin de Pré-Yonnet, which goes under the train tracks, then turn right onto Rue Margencel and right again onto Rue de la Gare, which of course takes you to the train station.

Montreux

You can lengthen this trip by getting onto national route #1 in Villeneuve (kilometer 5.6), which detours through the fields and villages along the Rhône, following it all the way to Aigle and adding about 9 km to your ride.

Château
de Chillon

Along the way

The first leg of this section is on Lake Geneva's quay of all quays. It runs for 7.2 km (you'll be doing 5.3 km of it) from the Port du Basset in Clarens, by the statue of Freddy Mercury in Montreux and right past the Château de Chillon, to Villeneuve at the southeast corner of the lake. While cycling is allowed, you need to keep your pace slow, because pedestrians have the right of way. There are many of them on sunny days, but it's worth the spectacular views of the lake and the adjoining luxury villas and apartments. As the signs say, *"cyclistes roulez au pas"* or, loosely translated, "cycle at walking speed".

Spend a few hours in the Château de Chillon, the 12th century fortress made famous by Lord Byron (look for his graffiti signature in the dungeon). The Château d'Aigle has a Vine, Wine and Label Museum that teaches you all about wine-making, from soil conditions to storing bottles.

Picnics are a breeze here, with plenty of supermarkets and shops for stocking up on supplies, and benches to sit on everywhere. Cafés and restaurants abound as well, and are of course perfect for trying out local wines. There is a public fire pit on the lake just before the Château de Chillon (kilometer 3.9).

Take-home specialties include l'Etivaz cheese brought down from the mountain in Château-d'Oex – and of course wine. For white, this is the home of Chasselas, Chardonnay and Sauvignon Blanc. The reds are less well-known but just as flavorful. Locals grow Pinot Noir and Gamay, as well as a bit of Gamaret, Garanoir and Merlot. The lovely towns of Yvorne and Aigle are major wine-tasting stops.

Swimming happens mostly in Lake Geneva, with free access here and there along the quay. Pools that charge admission for all the trimmings are the elegant Piscine du Casino in Montreux (one pool, lawn, terrace, parasols, cocktail lounge, VIP section, no lake access) and the more pedestrian Piscine communale Les Marines in Villeneuve (pool with lengths section, wading pool, diving towers in the lake, lawn, shade trees).

Hotel accommodations come in all ranges, from luxury and premium in Montreux to mid-range and camping in Villeneuve, through to boutique, mid-range and historical in Aigle.

Yvorne

AIGLE–MARTIGNY

Past tunnels in mountains to the central Valais gateway

VAUD, VALAIS

 START
Aigle

 FINISH
Martigny

 DISTANCE
32.22 km

 ELEVATION GAIN
63 m

 ASCENT
219 m

 DESCENT
156 m

 KID-FRIENDLY
yes

 TOURISM
aigle-leysin-lesmosses.ch

myswitzerland.com

martigny.com

 GPX TRACK
Flat Switzerland 12

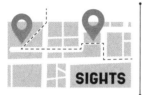

SIGHTS

salt mines in Bex, Grotte aux Fées, Abbey Saint-Maurice, Fondation Pierre Gianadda in Martigny

FOOD

cafés, restaurants, picnic areas

SPECIALTIES

Chasselas, salt from Bex, Raclette du Valais AOP, cornichons. See also Flat Switzerland 11

SWIMMING

Rhône, Piscine d'Aigle, Gouille de St Triphon, Lavey-les-Bains, Piscine Municipale Martigny

HOTELS

mid-range in Aigle and Martigny, budget in villages, premium thermal spa in Lavey-les-Bains

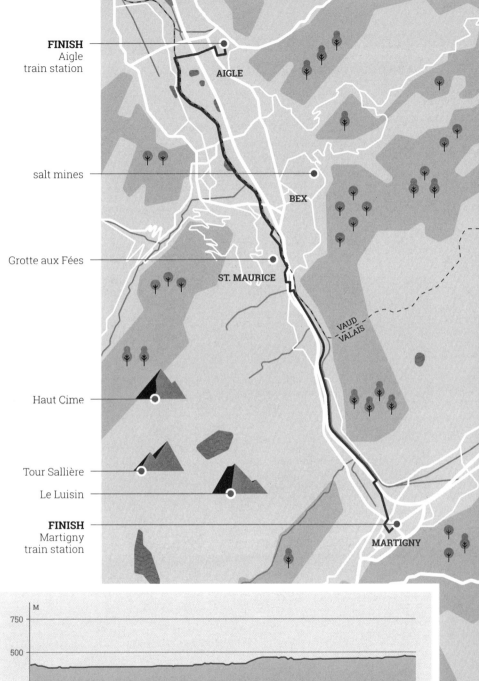

FINISH
Aigle
train station

AIGLE

salt mines

BEX

Grotte aux Fées

ST. MAURICE

VAUD
VALAIS

Haut Cime

Tour Sallière

Le Luisin

FINISH
Martigny
train station

MARTIGNY

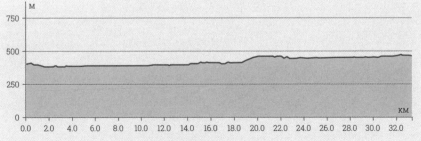

M
750

500

250

0
0.0 2.0 4.0 6.0 8.0 10.0 12.0 14.0 16.0 18.0 20.0 22.0 24.0 26.0 28.0 30.0 32.0
KM

Route description

Don't worry about leaving the wineries behind in Aigle –
there are more coming up ahead. The Rhône Valley gets
narrower here as the Dents du Midi and Dents de Morcles
mountain ranges rise up dramatically on either side, making
for some unnerving cliffscapes around Saint-Maurice (also
marked as St-Maurice on maps and road signs).

The directions for this section couldn't be easier: follow the
red national cycling signs for route #1 from Aigle to Martigny.

Along the way

If you have time, the still-active salt mines in Bex are a thrill. A tiny, quaky miner's train (there's just enough room in there for you to sit upright) takes you through hand-hewn tunnels deep into the mountain. Fascinating, but not for the claustrophobic. Get to the mine from Bex's train station by bus (on weekends) or taxi, or just hike the 4.6 km up to the entrance for some added exercise. Tours of the mines must be booked in advance.

©Altrendo Images

At kilometer 15.8, there's a 10-minute walking trail up to the entrance of the Grotte aux Fées, or Fairies' Grotto. Inside, you can follow about 600 meters of tunnels into the mountain to a small but spectacular subterranean lake with a 50 meter-high waterfall. It has been a tourist attraction since it was discovered in 1863.

Grottes aux Fées

Around the next bend, Saint-Maurice has a charming pedestrian main street running through its historic old town, with quite a few cafés and restaurants along it. The active Abbey of Saint-Maurice d'Agaune is just one street over to the west and has a restored 17th century basilica, an archeological exhibit, catacombs and a treasure room.

As an original site from the story of Zurich's patron Saints Felix and Regula, it can be of interest to visitors from Switzerland's largest city.

In Martigny, check to see what's on at the Fondation Pierre Gianadda: this cultural venue includes a collection of Impressionist painters, a Gallo-Roman museum built around the ruins of a temple and a Swiss car exhibit.

If you're not in the mood for a scenic *déjeuner sur l'herbe* on the banks the Rhône, the nicest restaurants in this region (after Aigle) line the Place Centrale in Martigny, which is dotted with seven rows of shade trees that run the length of the square and has lots of food options.

Saint-Maurice

As both the end of the line and a kind of link between the cantons of Vaud and Valais, Martigny (and Fully down the road) are great places to shop for specialties. Stock up on some Chasselas and local cornichons to go with an authentic Raclette du Valais AOP. You can pick up the potatoes from your hometown train station on your way back, or have them waiting for you in your cupboard.

Collonges

As most of this route runs along the Rhône, there are many opportunities to stop and jump in. But be cautious of the swift current, and the fact that the water may be colder than you expect if it is carrying a lot of glacier water; dip a toe in first. Fee-based swimming options are the Piscine d'Aigle (bathing, lengths, wading, playground, slide) and the Gouille de St Triphon, a swimming area with a snack bar on a small gravel-pit-turned-lake – and a slice of authentic reality at the edge of the freeway.

A bit more upscale is the Lavey-les-Bains thermal spa outside Saint-Maurice. It boasts two large pools (indoor, outdoor) and extras like hot tubs, jets, waterfalls, counter-current lanes, a sauna and hammam, Turkish baths and water fountains. The admission price is per hour.

But when you're hot and just want to cool down, the piscine Municipale Martigny community pool with slide, wading pool and lengths also does the trick.

Accommodations run from mid-range in Aigle and Martigny, budget in the smaller villages, and a premium thermal spa complex in Lavey-les-Bains.

MARTIGNY–SION

Let the wind push you up

VALAIS

START

Martigny

FINISH

Sion

SIGHTS Fondation Pierre Gianadda, Castles Valère and Tourbillon in Sion, Grotte St. Léonard

 DISTANCE

29.87 km

FOOD cafés, restaurants (international cuisines), picnic areas

ELEVATION GAIN

21 m

SPECIALTIES *lammlidji/geisslidji* (air-dried lamb/goat), asparagus, apricots, Pinot Noir & Humagne Rouge wines

ASCENT

122 m

DESCENT

101 m

SWIMMING Rhône, Piscine Municipale Martigny, Domaine des Îles in Sion, Bains de Géronde in Sierre

KID–FRIENDLY

yes

 TOURISM

martigny.com

siontourisme.ch

myswitzerland.com (search term "St-Léonard")

HOTELS mid-range, business and historical hotels throughout, stylish boutiques and historical hotels in Martigny, Sion and Sierre

 GPX TRACK

Flat Switzerland 13

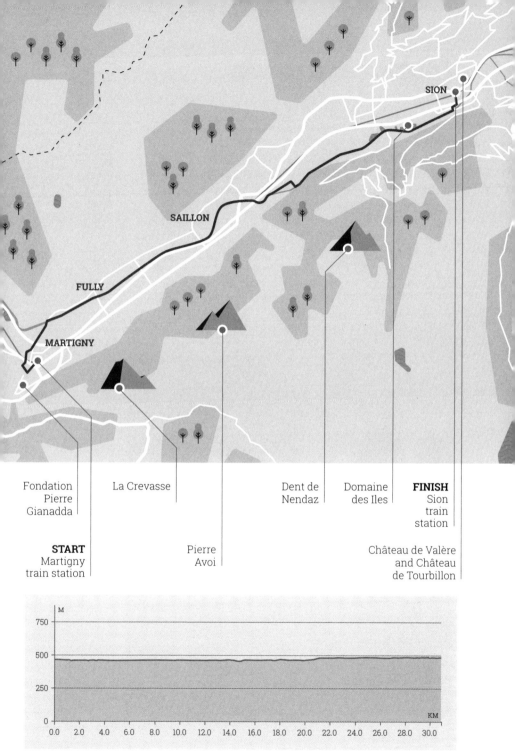

SION

SAILLON

FULLY

MARTIGNY

Fondation
Pierre
Gianadda

La Crevasse

Dent de
Nendaz

Domaine
des Iles

FINISH
Sion
train
station

START
Martigny
train station

Pierre
Avoi

Château de Valère
and Château
de Tourbillon

Route description

What was once a pretty scary ride on main roads is now a peacefully enjoyable outing along the banks of the Rhône. You probably won't notice much that you're going uphill: wind from Lake Geneva often picks up speed as it zips around the river bend in Martigny and blasts up the valley. This is also the reason why I don't recommend doing this route the other way, because you might end up cycling into headwinds that would have you standing on your pedals as you strain to cycle downhill.

The directions for this section are again very simple: just follow national cycling route #1 to Sion. Add an extra 19 km in distance and 37 m in altitude by carrying on to Sierre if you're feeling energetic. Its old-town charm is worth it.

Fully

Along the way

As discussed in Flat Switzerland 12, if you're so inclined it's worth having a look at what's being exhibited at the Fondation Pierre Gianadda in Martigny.

You'll mostly be riding beside the Rhône, so you might want to just enjoy the great Swiss outdoors: stunning Alps on either side of you, lines of poplars swaying in the wind, birds swirling overhead, all kinds of things buzzing and blooming in the grass, and the many trees, bushes and vines in the valley's fields growing much of the fruit and vegetables produced in Switzerland.

If you're looking for something solid, there's the 13th-century Château de Valère and its fortified church above Sion's old town, as well as the Château de Tourbillon on the opposite hill. Outside Sion on the hillside on the way to Sierre, you can take a guided boat ride on (but not actually swim in) the cool, beautiful underground lake in the Grotte St. Léonard (reservations required).

St-Pierre-de-
Clages

Either plan on shopping for picnic supplies in Martigny or Fully for one of the plentiful benches along the Rhône, or do side trips to the towns and villages to either side of the river – there are not many cafés or restaurants at its banks. See also the Le Domaine des Îles leisure park in the swimming section below.

As already introduced above, if Vaud and Valais fill many of the domestic wine aisles in Switzerland's supermarkets, this part of the valley is definitely responsible for much of its Swiss produce section. All kinds of fruit and vegetables are grown here, and the farmers of the Valais provide the majority of white asparagus, Williams pears – and apricots. In July and August you'll see apricot stands lining roads and on squares in front of train stations from Martigny to Brig. I almost always end up dragging a box of them home.

This is predominantly red wine country, with Pinot Noir at the top end of production. If you're looking for something a little different, try a glass of the lesser-known Humagne Rouge.

Arguably the most luxurious free swimming hole in Switzerland, and for many a destination in itself, the 133-acre Le Domaine des Îles leisure park at kilometer 26.7 has lawns, shade trees and access to a large lake. There is also a miniature train, tennis, mini-golf, wall climbing, beach volleyball and a fishing pond – some subject to a fee. A campground and restaurant are included on the grounds.

Chamoson

If you make it as far as Sierre, make sure you pack your swimsuit: its Bains de Géronde has two pools for splashing around, lengths and diving, a slide with its own "arrivals" pool, lawns, chairs, parasols and access to the large adjoining Lac de Géronde.

You'll find mid-range, business and historical hotels and camping throughout the region, with stylish boutiques and historical hotels in Martigny, Sion and Sierre.

LEUK–BRIG

An alpine valley with a Country & Western flair

VALAIS

Gestelnburg and Festiloch in Niedergesteln, Visp old town, side trip to Zermatt, old town and Stockalper Palace in Brig

cafés, restaurants, fire pits, picnic areas

air-dried beef, pork sausages, *génépi* schnaps, honey

Schwimmbad Mühleye, Brigerbad thermal baths and spa, Freibad Geschina

business and historical hotels, campgrounds with hut, tent and trailer rentals throughout the valley, stylish boutiques in Leuk, Visp and Brig

 START
Leuk

 FINISH
Brig

 DISTANCE
32.26 km

 ELEVATION GAIN
48 m

 ASCENT
165 m

 DESCENT
117 m

 KID-FRIENDLY
yes

 TOURISM
valais.ch

 GPX TRACK
Flat Switzerland 14

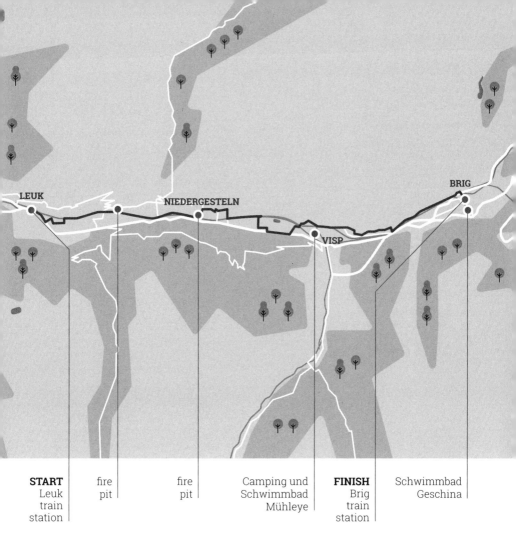

LEUK

NIEDERGESTELN

BRIG

VISP

START
Leuk
train
station

fire
pit

fire
pit

Camping und
Schwimmbad
Mühleye

FINISH
Brig
train
station

Schwimmbad
Geschina

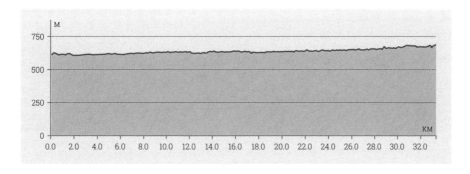

M

750

500

250

0

KM

0.0 2.0 4.0 6.0 8.0 10.0 12.0 14.0 16.0 18.0 20.0 22.0 24.0 26.0 28.0 30.0 32.0

Route description

You'll notice the air is a little drier in this section, a fact also reflected in the rocky landscape and the horse corrals here and there, which give it a Country & Western vibe.

If you're doing all of Flat Switzerland 10–14 over a few days or a week, either get on the local train with your bicycle in Sion (or Sierre) to Leuk – especially if you have kids with you – or continue to follow national cycling route #1. After Sierre, this will take you onto the main road through the Pfyn Forest to Leuk for about 7 kilometers, which really isn't any fun. On the other hand, you'll be able to brag you rode the whole way from Lausanne to Brig, so I'll leave it up to you to decide.

If you're starting in Leuk, follow national cycling route #1 to Brig.

Leuk

Along the way

The otherwise unassuming town of Niedergesteln has two nice sights. From the village church, scramble up Feschtiweg to the Gestelnburg ruins, which offer a nice view of the valley and the surrounding Alps. If you are not faint of heart, there's also a dry cave above the ruins called the *Festiloch* (fortress hole) dating back to the last ice age.

The narrow cobblestone alleys of Visp's hillside old town give it an Italian charm and hide all kinds of photogenic details – bring a good camera. The broader streets in Brig are conducive to strolling from shop to shop on your way to the central market square. The impressive Stockalper Palace, which was built by a 17th-century patrician, is a bit farther up the hill. Tours in English must be booked separately and run a bit high.

A side trip to Zermatt and Switzerland's unofficial trademark, the Matterhorn, is awfully tempting in Visp. A train leaves pretty much every half hour and gets you there in just over one.

Getwing

Cafés and restaurants are easy to find along the way. Most of all in the larger towns of Leuk, Visp and Brig. If you sit down for a meal (and you're new to the area and a meat-eater) order the local *Walliserteller* – air-dried beef, sausages, smoked bacon, local cheese, cornichons, pickled onions and in summer perhaps sliced tomatoes. Although this specialty can be found all over Switzerland, many of the best are found in this region.

You can gather supplies for picnics at the Leuk train station or in Gampel, Raron, Visp and Brig. Stores in villages tend to be closed over lunch.

There are two fire pits on the banks of the Rhône: one at kilometer 6.6 in Niedergampel and another at kilometer 11.6 in Niedergestein.

Aside from taking home local cheeses and dried charcuterie as souvenirs, try a jar of alpine honey or a bottle of *génépi* – a stiff, bitter, herb schnaps that's said to be good for your digestion. Or at least your mood.

As you move farther up the valley, swimming in the Rhône gets colder and more often swift currents make bathing dangerous. But there are fee-based *Badis*, one outside Visp at Camping und Schwimmbad Mühleye (pool, wading pool, slide, shade trees), and one in Brig called Schwimmbad Geschina with four pools (bathing with lengths section, slide, wading, diving).

The thermal baths and spa in Brigerbad offer no fewer than 12 pools at different temperatures and for various activities, with waterfalls, jets and underwater seating being just a few of the things that put the sound of "many" into the word amenities. There are also several restaurants, a campground and a long slide that runs down the hill above the compound and empties into its own pool. Prices are by the hour or the day.

Accommodations in the valley range from business and historical hotels to camping and trailer rentals. There are also stylish boutiques in Leuk, Visp and Brig.

Brigerbad

KANDERSTEG–SPIEZ

Through forests and meadows to Lake Thun

BERN

SIGHTS

Kandersteg, Oeschinensee, Blausee, Reichenbach i. K., Spiez lakeside and Schloss Spiez Museum

FOOD

cafés, restaurants, picnic areas

SPECIALTIES

Hobelkäse cheese, streusel cake, *Blauer Kuchen* puff pastries, *Murmeli-Kräutersalbe* lotion in Frutigen, Riesling-Sylvaner, Rosé and Pinot Noir wines in Spiez

SWIMMING

Schwimm- und Spielbad Kandersteg, Freibad Frutigen, Frei- und Seebad Spiez, Lake Thun

HOTELS

mid-range, historical hotels and B&Bs, plus chalets in Kandersteg, small resort at Blausee and premium in Spiez

 START
Kandersteg

 FINISH
Spiez

DISTANCE
31.47 km

 ELEVATION GAIN
-542 m

ASCENT
269 m

 DESCENT
811 m

 KID-FRIENDLY
yes

 TOURISM
kandersteg.ch

frutigen-tourismus.ch

thunersee.ch

 GPX TRACK

Flat Switzerland 15

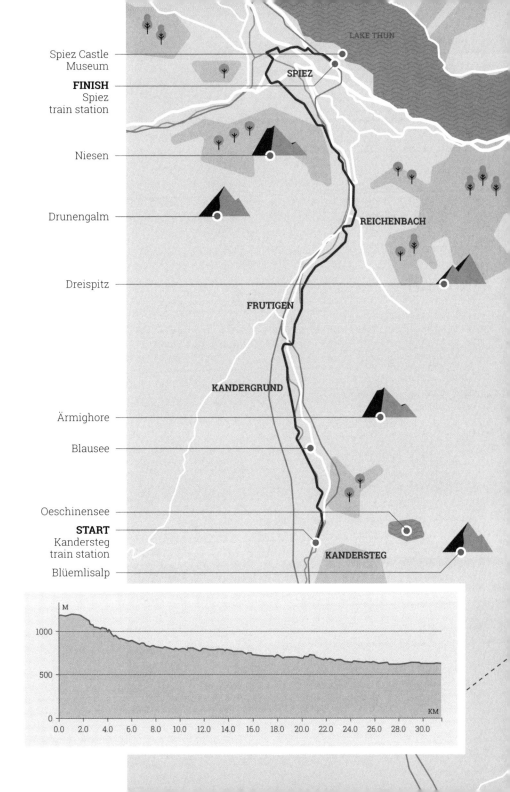

LAKE THUN

Spiez Castle
Museum

SPIEZ

FINISH
Spiez
train station

Niesen

Drunengalm

REICHENBACH

Dreispitz

FRUTIGEN

KANDERGRUND

Ärmighore

Blausee

Oeschinensee

START
Kandersteg
train station

KANDERSTEG

Blüemlisalp

M

1000

500

0

0.0 2.0 4.0 6.0 8.0 10.0 12.0 14.0 16.0 18.0 20.0 22.0 24.0 26.0 28.0 30.0

KM

Route description

The Kander Valley is one of the quietest in the Bernese Oberland, but there's a flip side hidden in its mountains: at the end of Kandersteg lies the Swiss Federal Council's official *Führungsanlage K20* escape bunker. Its formerly more-or-less secret location was revealed internationally in 2008, with coordinates listed on Wikipedia (they have since been removed). And it should be mentioned that there is a proposal to evacuate the nearby town of Mitholz for ten years so that a stockpile of unused WWII bombs can be transported from a military weapons dump deep inside the mountain to a safer disposal site elsewhere.

Little of this is noticeable to the untrained eye from outside, however. The valley and its scenic forests, Alps and postcard villages remain an open, vibrant local and international tourist destination.

From the Kandersteg train station, follow national cycling route #64 down the valley past Reichenbach and switch to route #9 at kilometer 26.4.

Kandersteg

Along the way

In Kandersteg, pick one of three gondolas up to the surrounding mountains – or all of the them, if you have the time. The sparkling Oeschinensee glacier lake and the Blüemlisalp massif it nests in are especially representative of everything the marketing term 'Swissness' stands for.

Blausee is a small private nature park and resort around the deep blue lake that gives it its name. It's a popular Sunday destination for Swiss tourists, who also come to lunch on trout organically farmed at the resort or overnight in the spa. Cross the little bridge over the Kander River at kilometer 5.2 and pay the park entrance fee at the hotel's reception desk.

Kandergrund

Before you start looking for the falls where Sherlock Holmes fell to his "death", those Reichenbach Falls are a few valleys over, east of Interlaken. But this Reichenbach is worth a stop because of the 18th-century chalets at the intersection of Dorfstrasse and Bahnhofstrasse at kilometer 17.9. One particularly stunning specimen even dates back to the 16th century and is helpfully now a gourmet restaurant.

Spiez Castle Museum offers history of the castle and the town of Spiez, as well as hosting changing art exhibits. The castle gardens are open to the public.

Kandersteg has a small local store if you're wanting to put together a picnic to eat on the way – there will certainly be enough striking spots to do so down the valley. Expect a few cafés and restaurants in local villages, but you'll find the most variety in Spiez.

The canton of Bern is of course a natural home to many dairy products, and this region has *Hobelkäse* – a hard cheese made to be cut paper-thin. If you're eating it soon, and want to slice the cheese as it is meant to be tasted, ask the store to do it for you or buy a cheese plane to take home. This is more precise than the spatula-like cheese slicer you may have in a drawer, and it makes a nice gift together with a block of the cheese.

Spiez

If you can get beyond what it's made of (chamois fat, olive oil and marmot oil), a big seller in Frutigen is *Murmeli-Kräutersalbe*, a balm for muscle and joint pain. Its ingredients are harvested sustainably from wild animals as part of the seasonal hunt in the local mountains.

The Kander River is quite chilly year-round, so unless you're a polar bear swim fan, try one of the aquatic centers like the Schwimm- und Spielbad Kandersteg (bathing, lengths, diving, wading and slide pools) or the Freibad Frutigen (bathing, lengths, partially shaded wading pool). Otherwise, wait until you reach Lake Thun and either "swim wild" or pay to get into the Frei- und Seebad Spiez (wading, diving, lengths, bathing, slide pools, lake access).

If you've never slept in a chalet, now's your chance. Kandersteg has a wide selection. There are also mid-range, historical hotels and B&Bs, as well as premium hotels in Spiez. The small Blausee resort has a spa with sauna, sanarium, "steaming grotto" and outdoor hot tubs.

SPIEZ-INTERLAKEN

A short ride along Lake Thun to Interlaken

BERN

SIGHTS

Schloss Spiez, Interlaken, Harder Kulm, Heimwehfluh, Eiger, Mönch, Jungfrau

FOOD

cafés, restaurants (international cuisines), picnic areas

SPECIALTIES

Spiezertorte almond chocolate pie, *Spiezer Bergsalami*, *Schlossbratwurst* with cherries, *Beatenberg Kräutertee* herbal tea

SWIMMING

Lake Thun, Frei- und Seebad Spiez, Freiluft- und Hallenbad Bödeli Interlaken Strandbad Bönigen, Lake Brienz

HOTELS

all ranges in Interlaken, mid-range, historical hotels and B&Bs and premium in Spiez. Camping in Interlaken.

 START

Spiez

 FINISH

Interlaken

 DISTANCE

19.31 km

 ELEVATION GAIN

-62 m

 ASCENT

138 m

 DESCENT

200 m

 KID-FRIENDLY

yes, but see Route description

 TOURISM

thunersee.ch

interlaken.ch

GPX TRACK

Flat Switzerland 16

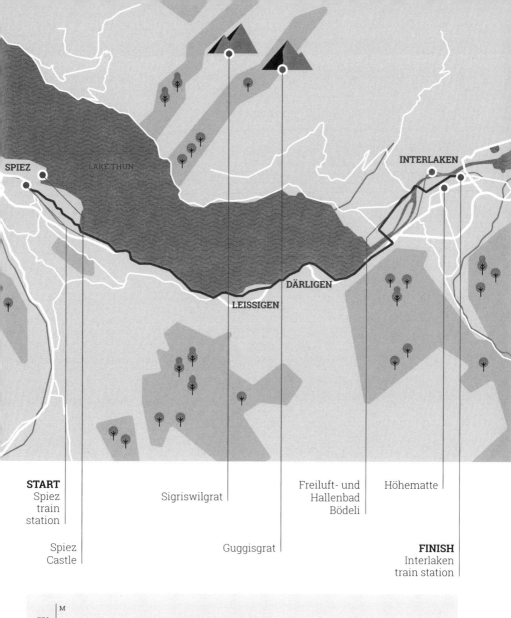

SPIEZ

LAKE THUN

INTERLAKEN

DÄRLIGEN

LEISSIGEN

START
Spiez
train
station

Sigriswilgrat

Freiluft- und
Hallenbad
Bödeli

Höhematte

Spiez
Castle

Guggisgrat

FINISH
Interlaken
train station

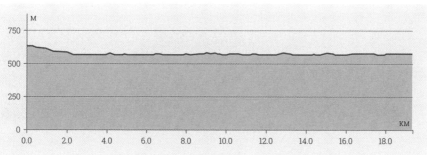

Route description

Once you've enjoyed all that Spiez has to offer, this easy ride is all about Lake Thun and Interlaken. It takes you through villages and the small lakeside parks between them to the historic center of one of Switzerland's first tourist towns.

Follow national cycling route #9 from Spiez to Interlaken Ost. If this is your first time here, please note that there are two train stations in Interlaken: Interlaken West, an intermediate station, and the Interlaken Ost terminus, where other lines go to Brienz, Lauterbrunnen, Wengen, Grindelwald, Mürren and the Jungfraujoch.

If you're bringing kids, there is one 2.5-km section between Därligen and the fields of Unterseen (kilometer 13 to 15.5) that runs along the main road, around a traffic circle and over a bridge before it goes back onto a quiet lane. It's a short section, but depending on their level of cycling experience, this may not be a route for them.

Along the way

Spiez Castle has a beautiful garden with benches and walkways overlooking its small bay, as well as a museum that will tell you all about the history of both the castle and the town.

Historically among the first tourist destinations in Switzerland, today's Interlaken is a town of contrasts. Older locals, families and international tourists stroll the town by day, while club kids crawl from one hotspot to the next by night. Hikers and cyclists travel on through; paragliders land on the grass of its large central park, Höhematte. Next to the elegant Victoria Jungfrau Grand Hotel & Spa, one of the 19th-century originals, there's a Hooters. And after more than 20 years in Interlaken, it's almost as much of an established tradition as its upper class neighbor.

Interlaken is a place to access boating on Lakes Thun and Brienz, and of course it's a starting point to the Eiger, Mönch and Jungfrau mountains. If you prefer a shorter trip with a view over Interlaken, take either the Heimwehfluhbahn funicular railway (about 500 m south of the Interlaken West train station) up to Heimwehfluh (elevation 662 m) or the Harderbahn (500 m from Interlaken Ost train station across the Beaurivage Bridge) to Harder Kulm (elevation 1322).

Spiez and, more so, Interlaken have large supermarkets with all the trimmings for your picnic – including that blanket you forgot. Especially in Interlaken, there are all kinds of cafés and restaurants, with all kinds of cuisines, from hamburgers and sushi to various Swiss specialties.

Lake Thun

If you're looking for something to take home, the town of Spiez produces some nice Riesling-Sylvaner, Rosé and Pinot Noir wines, and many wine shops ship. The most stores in Interlaken aimed at tourists are located between the main train stations Interlaken-West and Interlaken-Ost along Bahnhofstrasse and Höheweg, out to the edge of Höhematte Park. As a major destination, Interlaken has pretty much every type of visitor covered, so in addition to affordable Swiss watches and multifunctional pocket knives with Swiss crosses on them, you'll also find serious outdoor gear and sports equipment, as well as exorbitant "timepieces," jewelry, bags and other luxury goods. If you're looking for something to splurge on just this once, this is a place to do it.

The bay in Spiez gives you limited access to Lake Thun, but if you want more amenities, try the fee-based Frei- und Seebad Spiez (wading, diving, lengths, bathing, slide pools, lake access).

Once you've zipped from Spiez's train station down to Lake Thun, you'll see that each village – and sometimes spots in between – offer a bit of lawn to lie or picnic on before and after you go for a swim. Most of them look over to the green double mountain ridges Sigriswilgrat and Guggisgrat on the other side of the lake, with the Niederhorn looming over the town of Beatenberg.

The Freiluft- und Hallenbad Bödeli in Interlaken is a popular aquatic center, with one large pool with diving towers at one end, and a slide at the other, as well as a wading pool, lawns and shade trees. The *Strandbad* in Bönigen has three pools (including lengths and wading) plus lake access.

Finding accommodations along this route will not be an issue. Every town has at least historical hotels and B&Bs, Spiez includes a premium hotel and Interlaken offers all ranges, including several luxury properties and camping.

BRÜNIG–SARNEN

Through the forest, from lake to lake

BERN,
OBWALDEN

 START

Brünig-Hasliberg

SIGHTS

Brünig Brocki, Turrengrat mountain ridge, *Schwingen* wrestling events

 FINISH

Sarnen

 DISTANCE

23.49 km

FOOD

cafés, restaurants, fire pits, picnic areas

 ELEVATION GAIN

-529 m

▲ ASCENT

214 m

SPECIALTIES

Sbrinz AOP hard cheese, dried pears, *Öpfelauflauf* apple casserole, *Orangenmost* non-alcoholic orange cider

▼ DESCENT

743 m

 KID-FRIENDLY

yes

SWIMMING

Seepark Lungern, Lake Lungern, Seebad Bürglen, Strandbad Wilerbädli, Seefeld Park Sarnen, Lake Sarnen

 TOURISM

lungern-tourismus.ch

obwalden-tourismus.ch

HOTELS

historical hotels & B&Bs throughout, campgrounds in Lungern, Giswil and Sarnen

 GPX TRACK

Flat Switzerland 17

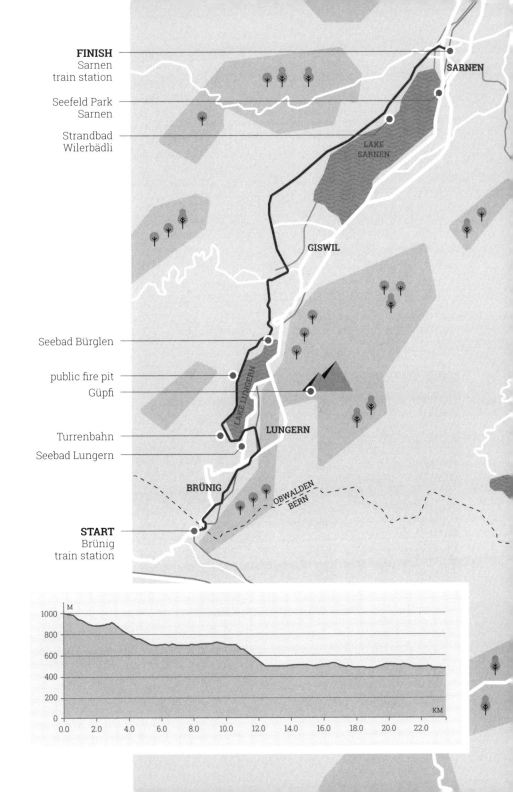

FINISH
Sarnen
train station

Seefeld Park
Sarnen

Strandbad
Wilerbädli

SARNEN

LAKE
SARNEN

GISWIL

Seebad Bürglen

public fire pit

Güpfi

LAKE LUNGERN

LUNGERN

Turrenbahn

Seebad Lungern

BRÜNIG

OBWALDEN
BERN

START
Brünig
train station

Route description

Just 500 meters after the Brünig-Hasliberg train station, national cycling route #9 leaves the main road, dropping you down into a rustic alpine valley surrounded by forest. At the end of it, at about kilometer 3, stop to admire the view of azure Lake Lungern 200 meters in elevation below you. The path then continues along the train tracks to the village of Lungern, then along the west side of Lake Lungern and Lake Sarnen for a quiet, picturesque ride through Central Switzerland. This route is easily combined with Flat Switzerland 18 for a full-day excursion.

If you're coming up by train from Brienz, be on the platform when it arrives to get yourself a spot for your bike; many tourists take the train from Interlaken to Luzern along this line.

Brünig

Lungern

Along the way

I sometimes have a hard time getting underway from the Brünig-Hasliberg station. Not only are there some good Swiss restaurants with views of the Aarboden Valley below, the station has a *Brocki* – a Swiss second-hand shop – attached to it. It's packed with agricultural, military and other Swiss antiques and old second-hand items that are fun to just look at. There's also a flea market in the town every 1st Sunday of the month.

This is a good area to experience outdoor Swiss wrestling, or *Schwingen*, which takes place up and down the valley and in Nidwalden from late spring to early fall (search keywords "Schwingen Obwalden" or see Obwalden Tourism).

Once you're down in Lungern, consider taking the
Turrenbahn up to the Turrengrat for a view over the valley.
If you're hungry already, there's a restaurant at the top
and three grated public fire pits with wood just 50 meters
northeast of the gondola station.

The whole valley is a local tourist destination. In summer
it's mostly about swimming, so you'll find a good number
of cafés, restaurants and picnic areas throughout. There's
another grated public fire pit with firewood at kilometer 8.2
on the shores of Lake Lungern.

A good souvenir to take home from Obwalden is the local Sbrinz AOP hard cheese, Switzerland's milder answer to Parmesan. Made from the milk of Brown Swiss cows fed only on grass in summer and hay in winter, it became a hit with northern Italians in the 16th century and is a popular grated cheese all over Switzerland.

Another good portable is *Orangenmost*. Even though it was invented in Beckenried, you're close enough to get this non-alcoholic cider made with oranges and apples in local stores. You can also try it first in cafés and restaurants.

Giswil

As the entrance to the great collection of large swimming holes that is Central Switzerland, there is lots of free access to both Lake Lungern and Lake Sarnen along this route. This includes the tiny Strandbad Wilerbädli at about kilometer 20.35 (at the end of the trail down to the lake). It has a lawn with a shade tree and provides free umbrellas, showers, toys for kids, as well as a raft out on the lake. You can purchase food and drinks at the attached kiosk, which is open if the Swiss flag on the roof is up.

The *Badi* in Lungern is called Seepark Lungern. It has a strip of lawn with a few shade trees, a bit of sandy beach for the kiddies and a decent slide. Most of the excitement happens out on the lake, thanks to a couple of swim rafts and a diving tower with another slide. You can rent pedalos, SUPs and kayaks.

At the northern end of the lake, Seebad Bürglen is free (but asks for donations) and provides a grated fire pit, picnic tables and bathrooms.

The Seefeld Park Sarnen aquatic center has a large lawn with shade trees, wading pool, playground and lake access, an outdoor pool with water features and an open-roofed indoor pool with a lengths section. The center has an attached campground.

For overnights, the valley offers historical hotels and B&Bs, with camping in Lungern, Giswil and Sarnen.

Bürglen

SARNEN–LUZERN

A meadow-to-lake flatliner

OBWALDEN,
NIDWALDEN,
LUZERN

 START

Sarnen

SIGHTS Mount Pilatus,
Glasi Hergiswil,
Luzern

 FINISH

Luzern

 DISTANCE

26.85 km

FOOD cafés, restaurants
(international cuisine),
firepit, picnic areas

 ELEVATION GAIN

-38 m

 ASCENT

129 m

SPECIALTIES *Bätziwasser* schnaps,
Birähung pear honey (Sarnen);
Birrewegge pear pastry,
Chriesisuppe cherry soup,
Chatzestreckerli biscuits (Luzern)

 DESCENT

167 m

 KID– FRIENDLY

yes

SWIMMING Ufschötti and Lido Luzern
on Lake Lucerne

 TOURISM

obwalden-
tourismus.ch

luzern.com

 GPX TRACK

Flat Switzerland 18

HOTELS limited in Sarnen;
all categories in Luzern

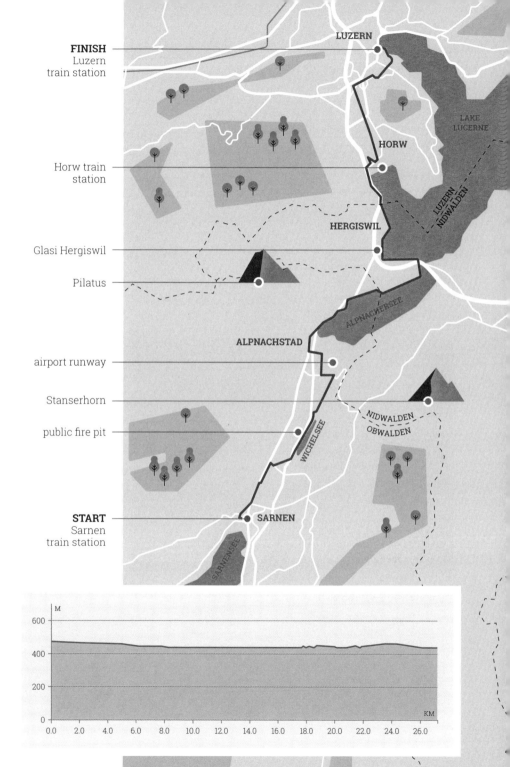

FINISH
Luzern
train station

LUZERN

HORW

LAKE
LUCERNE

Horw train
station

LUZERN
NIDWALDEN

HERGISWIL

Glasi Hergiswil

Pilatus

ALPNACHERSEE

ALPNACHSTAD

airport runway

Stanserhorn

NIDWALDEN

public fire pit

OBWALDEN

WICHELSEE

START
Sarnen
train station

SARNEN

SARNENSEE

Route description

Cruise through lush, yodely Swissness (and underneath some amazing granite cliff engineering) to one of the country's biggest tourist spots. Stop for a beer, nap it off, pedal some more, cool off with a swim. Bliss.

Getting to or back from Sarnen has a tricky side to it: unless you live in Sarnen or Luzern, have cycled here from somewhere else, or have a support team bringing you by car, timing is everything to get your bike here. The easiest way is by local train from/to Luzern, but this tends to be full of commuters during rush hour and tourists from April to September. It's best to go in late morning – and to get to the train early to make sure there's a spot for your bike.

Elevated
freeway
outside
Hergiswil

Another option is to combine this with the Brünig-Sarnen leg (Flat Switzerland 17) and bring a bike from Interlaken – here as well you need to watch out for trains full of tourists. Time of day won't make much of a difference because it's not a commuter route, but again: get to the train well in advance and grab a spot for your bike.

Alpnachstad

Follow national cycling route #9 to the outskirts of Horw until about kilometer 20.6. There, ignore the #9 turn and continue straight along Brünigweg to kilometer 21.1, where it turns into Wegmattstrasse and swerves left. At Technikumstrasse, turn right and right again at the roundabout on Ringstrasse, go under the railroad bridge and at the next roundabout on the other side turn left onto Allmendstrasse, which turns into Brändistrasse, then left onto Schäferweg up to the old railway line, which has been converted into the Freigleis cycling path. Take that to Sternmattstrasse and turn right, then left at Fruttstrasse to the bridge, then left again to the underpass beneath the bridge and follow Güterstrasse-Rösslimattweg, turn right into Rösslimattstrasse, left on Werkhofstrasse, left on Landenbergstrasse, left on Werftestrase, then follow Inseliquai and you'll find yourself at the lake's edge in front of the train station.

There's an added thrill at kilometer 7 just before Alpnachstad: you'll be crossing a light-aircraft runway. But this is Switzerland, so you're safe. They have installed a stoplight to keep you from getting smeared by any plane on its way in for a landing.

Along the way

It's hard to cycle through Alpnachstad and not be tempted by the cogwheel train up to Mount Pilatus, where the view is awesome on a clear day and there's an outdoor terrace to lounge on. The train takes 20 minutes each way.

The bike trail is out in the countryside mostly, but reconnects with typical Swiss cuisine and the odd international fare in Sarnen, Alpnachstad, Hergiswil, Horw and Luzern.

There is a grated fire pit at Wichelsee (kilometer 4.3) with a woodpile and picnic tables. All you need are matches and food to grill. The lake and its surroundings are part of a nature preserve though, so you can't swim in it.

The Hergiswil Glasi glass works are easy to visit – you'll be cycling right past the front door. Both store and museum celebrate the art of glassmaking, and they ship to your home so that any purchase you may make won't break on the back of your bicycle. Luzern is the spot for Swiss souvenirs of all types and price ranges. The most touristy is Grendelstrasse. From there you can head into the old town, where locals shop too.

Lake Lucerne has many opportunities for swimming, it basically being one big pool. The official, boat-free spots are the Ufschötti on the southwestern side, which is free and has just a kiosk and showers, and the Lido directly across, which offers a multitude of amenities with admission.

While at time of writing hotels were sparse in Sarnen, it will come as no surprise that Luzern has several to choose from for every pocketbook, style and level of happiness – with hotels running the gambit from 19th century grandes dames to 21st century boutiques.

Bonus question: "Lucerne" or "Luzern"? Since the British defined Switzerland as a tourist destination and used the French version of place names no matter which language region they were in, most towns and cantons have switched back to local usage in English. Except where the French version is internationally established – like in the case of "Lake Lucerne". For an extra helping of confusion, the tourist office uses both versions, but to locals it's "Luzern".

Luzern

LUZERN–ZUG

An urban-rural mix with villas, cows and golf

LUZERN,
ZUG

SIGHTS Old towns Luzern & Zug, Jesuitenkirche Luzern

FOOD cafés, restaurants (international cuisine), fire pits, picnic areas

SPECIALTIES *Pastetli* Luzern, lake fish, *kirsch*, *Zuger Kirschtorte*; *Tuusig-Bohne-Ragout* with peas, lentils, Entlebucher sausages, lamb, bacon, potatoes, *Kafi Luz* coffee with a shot of pear schnaps

SWIMMING Reuss River, Reusszopf Park, Strandbad Hünenberg, Hirsgarten Cham, Siehbach Bad, Seebad Seeliken

HOTELS all categories in Luzern and Zug, midrange, business hotels and B&B in between

 START
Luzern

 FINISH
Zug

 DISTANCE
30.73 km

 ELEVATION GAIN
-15 m

 ASCENT
223 m

DESCENT
238 m

 KID-FRIENDLY
yes

TOURISM
luzern.com
zug-tourismus.ch

 GPX TRACK
Flat Switzerland 19

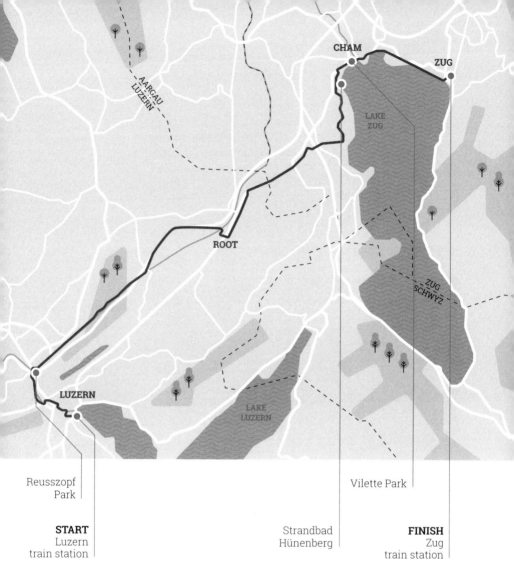

AARGAU
LUZERN

CHAM

ZUG

LAKE
ZUG

ROOT

ZUG
SCHWYZ

LUZERN

LAKE
LUZERN

Reusszopf
Park

Vilette Park

START
Luzern
train station

Strandbad
Hünenberg

FINISH
Zug
train station

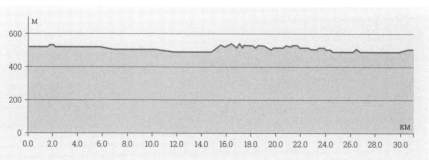

Route description

Between the small cities of Luzern and Zug lie glimpses of Swiss suburbia near the wooded banks of the Reuss River, followed by long stretches of pretty pastures, gated luxury properties and suddenly, a golf course. The influence of gradually encroaching metropolitan Zurich is evident, but the ride is still enjoyably refreshing.

Follow the red signs for national cycling route #9 from Luzern's train station to the one in Zug.

Along the way

If you have something with you to cover your cycling shorts, stop in at the 16th-century Jesuitenkirche in Luzern. The restored interior of this exceptional baroque church is reminiscent of white wedding cake frosting with pink and gilded highlights. The monumental frescoes on the ceiling tell the story of the church's patron saint, Francis Xavier.

Luzern

Luzern's famous old town is not only beautiful to look at, it's also home to regular shopping for locals and tourists alike. Bring home *Chatzestreckerli* biscuits (see also Flat Switzerland 18) as souvenirs from one of the many bakeries. Otherwise shop for yourself: there are all kinds of stores and their location in the center of town is very practical. The end of Grendelstrasse towards Schwanenplatz has the most souvenir shops for all budgets.

The closer you get to Zug, the more hedges there are to almost hinder you from gawping at the villas behind them. Sometimes the open gates are enticing. Many of the properties that have direct access to Lake Zug from Hünenberg to Zug are privately owned. But this is also a local destination for walks and cycling behind the villas along the train tracks, and lake swimming in between – thanks to public parks and *Badis*. Especially notable is the large Vilette Park, which includes a restaurant in the former villa, two playgrounds – one for smaller kids with sand, swings and a slide, and one for the older ones with a large wooden train to climb all over. It also offers lots of grass and benches to picnic on.

Freudenberg

Order the *Pastetli* if you feel like going out to eat in Luzern. This specialty made of finely ground beef and pork balls in cream sauce is served in a puff pastry cup. A quick *Kafi Luz* – coffee with a shot of pear schnaps – is a local pick-me-up. In Zug, the quintessential dessert is a piece of *Zuger Kirschtorte* – a cake made with hazelnuts and dribbled with *Kirsch*, the regional cherry schnaps. Better yet, take a *Zuger Kirschtorte* (or a bottle of *Kirsch*) home from one of the bakeries nearby. Lake trout and perch are a specialty in both cities.

For a picnic along the Reuss River that involves grilling, there's a public fire pit at kilometer 5.7.

The old town of Zug is smaller than the one in Luzern, but has a big square by the lake surrounded by strategically placed restaurants, as well as small specialty and gift shops along its cobblestone streets.

Once you get to Reusszopf Park at kilometer 3.7, you can swim almost anywhere along the Reuss (exceptions are before two small dams, both signposted). You'll find *Badis* for lazy lakeside lounging at Strandbad Hünenberg (pool without lengths, wading pool, shaded playground, lake access, diving tower in the lake, lawns, shade trees), and free lake access at Hirsgarten Cham (showers, big lawn), Strandbad Seeweg in Cham (pool without lengths, wading pool, shaded playground, lawns, shade trees, lake access, diving tower in the lake, swim rafts; this *Badi* may charge admission in future), Siehbach Bad in Zug (lawn, shades trees) and Seebad Seeliken in Zug (lawn, shade trees, wooden dock, swim raft).

Hotels are easy to find along this route, with all categories in Luzern and Zug, as well as mid-range and business hotels and B&Bs in between.

Hirsgarten,
Cham

ZUG–BRUNNEN

Along lakes and fields to the roots of Switzerland

ZUG,
SCHWYZ

 START

Zug

SIGHTS

Zug old town, Natur-
und Tierpark Goldau,
Schwyz town hall murals,
Mount Rigi

 FINISH

Brunnen

 DISTANCE

30.64 km

FOOD

cafés, restaurants
(international in Zug),
fire pit, picnic areas

 ELEVATION GAIN

14 m

SPECIALTIES

Kirsch schnaps,
Zuger Kirschtorte,
Gubel-Krapfen (cookies
with hazelnut filling)

 ASCENT

227 m

 DESCENT

213 m

SWIMMING

Seebad Seeliken, Badestelle
Tellenörtli Oberwil bei Zug,
Badi Trubikon, Seebad Arth,
Camping/Seebad Buchenhof,
Seebad Seewen,
Strandbad Hopfräbe Brunnen,
Lidopark Brunnen

 KID-FRIENDLY

no, see Route
description

 TOURISM

zug-tourismus.ch

schwyz-
tourismus.ch

HOTELS

all categories in Zug, up to
premium in Brunnen and
mid-range, business hotels
and B&Bs in between

 GPX TRACK

Flat Switzerland 20

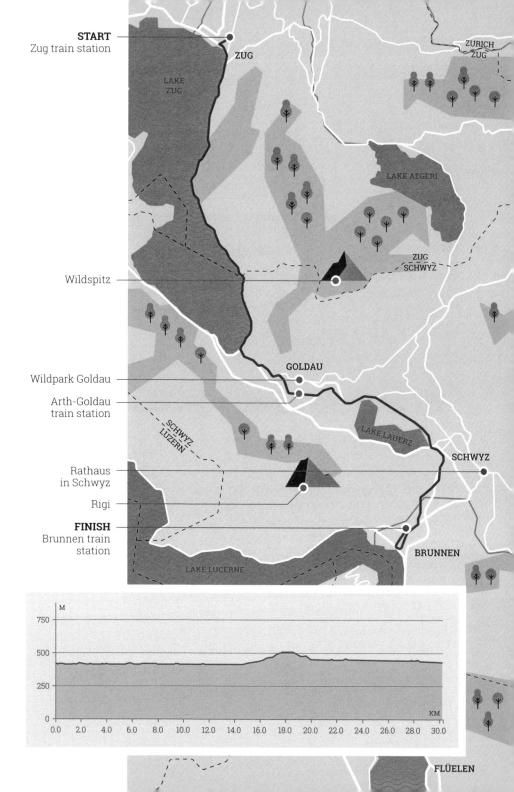

START
Zug train station

ZUG

LAKE
ZUG

ZURICH
ZUG

LAKE AEGERI

ZUG
SCHWYZ

Wildspitz

GOLDAU

Wildpark Goldau

Arth-Goldau
train station

SCHWYZ
LUZERN

Rathaus
in Schwyz

SCHWYZ

LAKE LAUERZ

Rigi

FINISH
Brunnen train
station

BRUNNEN

LAKE LUCERNE

FLÜELEN

M
750

500

250

0
0.0   2.0   4.0   6.0   8.0   10.0   12.0   14.0   16.0   18.0   20.0   22.0   24.0   26.0   28.0   30.0

KM

Route description

With its "mini-downtown" – just a few square blocks of squat glass-and-steel business towers – adjoining a small medieval old town, Zug reflects the transition from the eastern Swiss commercial region to the green meadows and mountains of the country's center, where Switzerland has its historic roots.

Zug

From the western exit of Zug's train station along Albisstrasse, follow the red signs for regional cycling route #58 south to the lake. After a few twists and turns through the old town, it takes you to a bicycle lane on the main lakeshore road, and at kilometer 2.3 it switches to the sidewalk shared with pedestrians along much of Lake Zug. But after kilometer 9.2 there is a 6.5-km section where the bicycle lane is again directly on the road. For this reason, I would not recommend this route for small children.

At kilometer 26.7, keep an eye out for the route #77 sign to Brunnen. You'll want to go past Brunnen's train station and ride down to the lakeshore (about 500 meters, just follow the *Flat Switzerland 20* GPX track to its end) to take in the view for the full Swissness effect. In German we call what you see to the right the Vierwaldstättersee (Lake of Four Forest Cantons) and to the left the Urnersee (Lake Uri). In English the whole thing is generally called "Lake Lucerne".

If you turn left at Brunnen's harbor along Axenstrasse, after about 500 meters you'll see a red cycling sign affixed to the right side of the beginning of a tunnel over the road. This is essentially a "cycle at your own risk" warning. An additional 12 km along the lake to Flüelen offers great views of the lake and goes through the historical, hand-hewn tunnels formerly used by carriages and cars until about 1940. But as a cyclist, for most of the way you have to ride in a bicycle lane on a modern road that is already dangerous to cars, given the heavy traffic and frequent landslides. It is even more so if you're on a bike, since you also share the road with trucks for at least 6 kilometers, often through exhaust-laden, modern tunnels. The safest way to see the historical tunnels is to take the boat or train to Flüelen and walk the *Weg der Schweiz* trail northwards from there to the Axenegg viewpoint (about 4 km) or all the way back to Brunnen (12 km).

Old
Axenstrasse

Along the way

In addition to the lake, the big draw in Zug is a few hours of wandering around its old town, which is compact and full of food options and specialty shops.

Wildpark Goldau is stocked with approximately 100 native Swiss and European animals and is popular for family outings.

On the façade of the *Rathaus* (town hall) in Schwyz, impressive murals illustrate legends and actual historical events from the 12th and 13th centuries surrounding the birth of Switzerland.

At the Arth-Goldau train station, a cogwheel train takes you up to the top of Mount Rigi in 44 minutes for a gorgeous view of the surrounding countryside – weather permitting.

Zug has the most variety of cafés and international restaurants, as well as large supermarkets for stocking up on picnic supplies. Zug's lakeshore is dotted with small parks and benches for a pit stop. The route's villages mostly specialize in Swiss fare, and for locals, Brunnen is a popular destination for lunches with a view of Lake Lucerne. There's a lakeside public fire pit in the free Badestelle Tellenörtli in Oberwil bei Zug at kilometer 3.7.

Unteregg

If you're looking for something to take home, try the *Gubel-Krapfen* (cookies with hazelnut filling) in one of Zug's local bakeries. Or of course a piece of the famous *Zuger Kirschtorte* combined with a bottle of *Kirsch* schnaps itself.

In addition to the wild swimming options along Lake Zug, there are free parks at Badestelle Tellenörtli and Badi Trubikon in Oberwil bei Zug (lawns, shade trees, changing rooms, bathrooms), as well as one on Lake Lucerne at the Lidopark Brunnen (lawn, shade trees).

Fee-based lake access includes Seebad Arth on Lake Zug (lawn, shade trees, diving tower, water features in park for kids), Camping/Seebad Buchenhof (lawn, shade trees, swim raft) and Seebad Seewen (lawn, shade trees, diving tower, swim raft) on Lake Lauerz, and Strandbad Hopfräbe Brunnen (lawn, shade trees, swim raft, wading pool with slide) on Lake Lucerne.

Hotels are easy to find along this route, with all categories in Zug, up to premium in Brunnen, as well as mid-range and business hotels, B&Bs and camping in between.

AIROLO–BELLINZONA

From Alps to palm trees

TICINO

SIGHTS

Piumogna waterfall outside Faido, San Nicolao church in Giornico, Bellinzona castles

FOOD

grocery stores, picnics in the wild, cafés and restaurants

SPECIALTIES

salami, *amaretti*, honey, goat cheese, merlot, *grappa nocino*, see also Flat Switzerland 22

SWIMMING

Ticino River

HOTELS

sparse and generally small, but there are a few smart, polished hotels on offer

 START
Airolo

 FINISH
Bellinzona

 DISTANCE
64.62 km

 ELEVATION GAIN
-978 m

 ASCENT
283 m

 DESCENT
1261 m

 KID-FRIENDLY
no

 TOURISM
ticino.ch

 **GPX TRACK**
Flat Switzerland 21

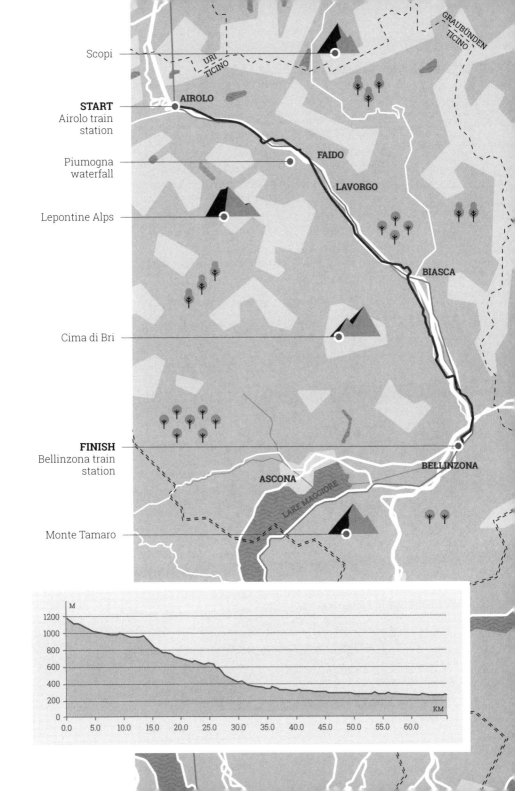

Route description

One of the most dramatic routes in Switzerland, this section has been traditionally used for team-building exercises since at least the early 90s – when people hoisted themselves onto rigid racing bikes and zoomed flat-out down the valley on the main road to Biasca (What's a helmet?) to have spaghetti, beer and a cigarette.

These days, cyclists are arguably healthier and bicycles safer. The route now often splits off onto calmer side roads and wooded paths, and it has been extended to Ascona for those who, literally, have all day. We will concentrate on getting to Bellinzona.

Because you will still mainly be sharing the road with local traffic not taking the freeway down the valley, this route is not recommended for kids or beginners.

Airolo

Biaschina
Viaduct

By the end of this route you'll have cycled up a cumulative 283 meters. But it is and certainly feels downhill all the way from Airolo, with the first 30 km dropping you about 600 meters into the valley. The most impressive descent comes after Lavorgo at kilometer 27.4, with two hairpin turns that wind their way down 40 meters. If that isn't dramatic enough for you, look up: the Biaschina Viaduct freeway bridge is right there looming over you, 110 meters above the valley floor.

You'll be following the red signs of national cycling route #3, so this route is easy to navigate. And as long as you're going downhill before Biasca, you'll know you're heading in the right direction. There the Ticino valley bends to the south, with the route passing over the freeway towards Iragna and onwards down to Bellinzona.

Along the way

San Nicolao in Giornico is one of Switzerland's most beautiful Romanesque churches and the oldest in Ticino. Once a Cluniac Benedictine monastery, it is well worth a visit thanks to the 13th century frescoes by Nicolao da Seregno. As is the picturesque town itself. When you stand bathed in its quiet charm, it's hard to imagine that in 1478 the town was the site of a battle – during which around 600 local soldiers, outnumbered by about 20-to-one, took advantage of snow conditions and the boulders around them and pushed the Duke of Milan's army back down the valley to his stronghold in Bellinzona.

Part of the UNESCO World Heritage, the three castles of
Bellinzona stand guard over a charming old town. The
largest and closest, Castelgrande, has an elevator that takes
you up from the Piazza Collegiata town square. Montebello,
and above that Sasso Corbaro, will take a little more work:
cycle up the road starting from Via Daro on the southeast
side of the train station or hike through the vineyards
(follow the yellow hiking signs from the station) for a
gorgeous view of the valley.

Your best bets for grocery stores, cafés and restaurants
are in Airolo, Faido, Biasca and Bellinzona, and there are
roadside eateries aimed at cyclists in Piotta and Ambrì
as well. Otherwise there are some lovely off-piste picnic
options next to fields, woods and the river between Faido
and Lavorgo, Giornico and Biasca, as well as Iragna and
Bellinzona.

Souvenirs from Ticino means food: my favorite of all the
gourmet highlights from the region is *nocino*, a dark brown
liqueur made from green walnuts that has a slightly bitter
taste to go with its nuttiness. See also Flat Switzerland 22
for more specialties.

The Ticino river is cool in summer but that's a good thing
on a hot day. Dip into one of the pools formed by the iconic
Ticinese granite boulders. Stand under the gorgeous,
43-meter high Piumogna waterfall just across the river from
Faido off kilometer 19.2 – only a 5-minute detour from the
cycling path.

While this region was a tourist destination in itself at the
turn of the 20th century, as evidenced by the once grand
former hotels and liberty style houses that dot the roads,
most travelers today head straight for Ascona or Lugano.
This has had a negative effect on local accommodations
in upper Ticino. But although they are few in number and
generally small, you can find smart, polished hotels on offer
between Airolo and Bellinzona.

Giornico

BELLINZONA– LOCARNO VIA ASCONA

Dolce far niente in the summer alpine sun

TICINO

SIGHTS

Bellinzona castles, Madonna del Sasso, Locarno old town, Ascona promenade

FOOD

cafés, restaurants, picnic areas

SPECIALTIES

coppa, lardo, pancetta, loto rice, polenta, see also Flat Switzerland 21

SWIMMING

Lido Locarno, Lido Ascona

HOTELS

mid-range, business hotels and B&Bs, camping, premium in Locarno, premium and luxury in Ascona

 START
Bellinzona

 FINISH
Locarno

 DISTANCE
33.77 km

 ELEVATION GAIN
-36 m

 ASCENT
157 m

 DESCENT
193 m

 KID-FRIENDLY
yes

 TOURISM
ticino.ch

 GPX TRACK
Flat Switzerland 22

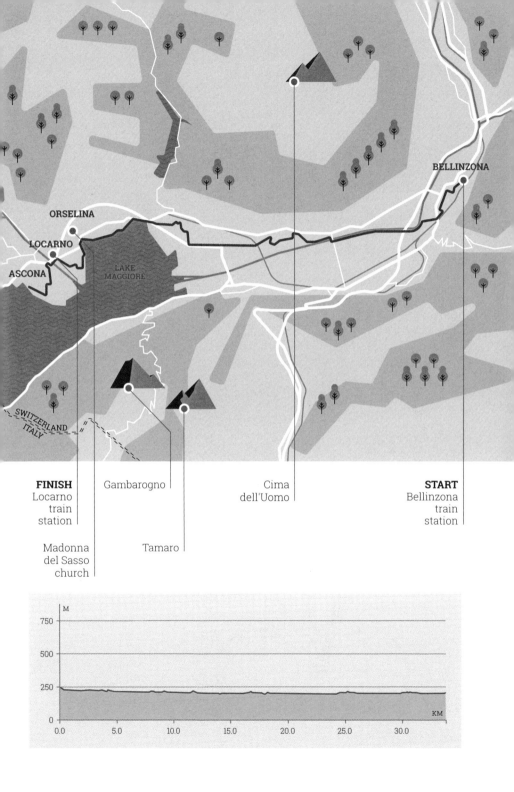

BELLINZONA

ORSELINA

LOCARNO

ASCONA

LAKE
MAGGIORE

SWITZERLAND
ITALY

FINISH
Locarno
train
station

Gambarogno

Madonna
del Sasso
church

Tamaro

Cima
dell'Uomo

START
Bellinzona
train
station

Route description

Another easy cycle in terms of directions. You're basically riding along the river to Lago Maggiore, so you'd have to try very hard to get lost. From Bellinzona's train station, follow the red signs for regional cycling route #31 to Ascona, passing through Locarno (you'll return there to catch the train, as Ascona doesn't have a station). Route #31 splits at kilometer 25.2 (up the Maggia River and down to Ascona's promenade) – follow the signs to Ascona. Once you're ready to go home, follow route #31 back to Locarno's train station.

At kilometer 18.6 you will be on the promenade along Lago Maggiore. You'll share the path with pedestrians, so the speed limit in this section is 5 km/h, but the views are worth it and this book is about not being in a hurry anyway. Should you prefer to go faster and ride through the residential streets of Minusio and Muralto instead, you can split off at kilometer 19. If you decide to do that, head back to the lake by rejoining route #31 after the train station in Locarno.

Castelgrande,
Bellinzona

Along the way

In Bellinzona you can't miss the three UNESCO-listed castles – Castelgrande, Montebello and Sasso Corbaro. The closest to the center, Castelgrande, can be reached on foot (there will be stairs) from Piazza Orico via Salita al Castelgrande, past gardens and small vineyards. But there's also an elevator up from Piazza del Sole if you're feeling a bit more leisurely.

Another opportunity for a nice 20-minute hike up quite a few stairs is the Madonna del Sasso church in Orselina. The path follows the stations of the cross and rewards you with a stunning view of Locarno and Lago Maggiore. A funicular up the hill starts across the street from Locarno's train station.

If you prefer to remain at ground level, the lakeshore in Muralto, Locarno's old town and Ascona's promenade provide a full-on Italianate feeling, even if you're only here for the day. Palm trees, sparkling blue water, an outdoor table on cobblestones in the sunshine – is there anything more you need?

The old town of Bellinzona features cafes, restaurants, department stores, as well as small specialty and gift shops along its cobblestone streets. Your basket will be full and the best picnic spots start with the promenade along Lago Maggiore at kilometer 18.6. As tourist destinations, Locarno and Ascona have a wide range of eating options that feature outdoor seating and skew towards Ticinese and Italian cuisine.

Continuing the list begun in Flat Switzerland 21, food specialties in Ticino make perfect souvenirs, among them coppa, lardo, pancetta, polenta – and loto rice. The latter is grown on a small farm on the Maggia delta in Ascona (turn left at kilometer 26.2, the fields start just after Via Muraccio).

Progero

Locarno and Ascona are prime swimming destinations. As if plentiful, free access to the gorgeous Lago Maggiore from the many lakeside parks weren't enough, both towns feature extravagant swimming facilities. Lido Locarno is an aquatic center with two pools (lengths, fitness), a gym and a spa indoors, five pools outdoors (bathing, lengths, diving, wading with water features, thermal), including four slides and sprawling lawns, 5,400 square meters of shade trees, and a sandy beach with swim rafts.

If Locarno's *lido* is all about exercise, the Lido Ascona is a lakeside lounge for the *dolce far niente* set. Swim out to the inflatable rafts, lie around on the lawn, have lunch, have a drink in the seating area and listen to the smooth musical stylings of the in-house DJ. If all you've brought is your wallet, you can buy bathing suits, towels, sunscreen and anything else you need for the afternoon at the *lido*'s shop. Should you insist on being energetic, you can rent SUPs or pedalos, or let yourself be pulled around on a wakeboard or banana boat.

Hotels in this region cover everything from mid-range and business hotels and B&Bs (Bellinzona), including premium in Locarno, and premium and luxury in Ascona. There is camping on the eastern end of Lago Maggiore and next to the Lido Locarno, though in the high season they can fill up.

Locarno

Lido Ascona

ZUG–ZURICH

A cool, protected forest between two cities

ZUG,
ZURICH

SIGHTS

Sihlwald forest, *Wildnispark Zürich Langenberg*, Zurich

FOOD

cafés, restaurants (international cuisine), picnic areas

SPECIALTIES

Bärlauch (wild garlic), *Zürcher Geschnetzeltes* (sliced veal in mushroom cream sauce), *Luxemburgerli* (light macarons), *Wiedikerli* sausages, see also Flat Switzerland 19 and 20

SWIMMING

Sihl River, Mythenquai, Tiefenbrunnen, Zürihorn on Lake Zurich

HOTELS

all categories in Zug and Zurich, camping in between

 START

Zug

 FINISH

Zurich

 DISTANCE

31.77 km

 ELEVATION GAIN

-12 m

 ASCENT

243 m

 DESCENT

255 m

 KID-FRIENDLY

no, 6 km along the main road

 TOURISM

zug-tourismus.ch

zuerich.com

GPX TRACK

Flat Switzerland 23

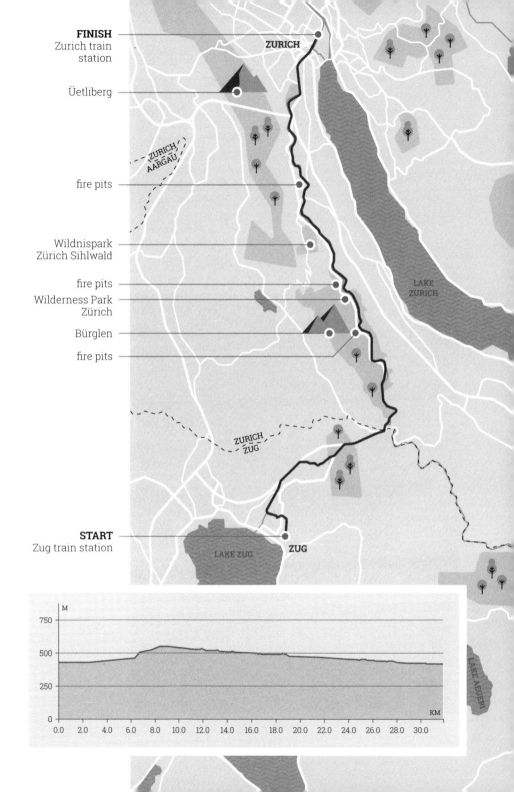

FINISH
Zurich train station

ZURICH

Üetliberg

ZURICH
AARGAU

fire pits

Wildnispark
Zürich Sihlwald

fire pits

Wilderness Park
Zürich

Bürglen

fire pits

LAKE
ZURICH

ZURICH
ZUG

START
Zug train station

LAKE ZUG

ZUG

LAKE AEGERI

M																
750
500
250
0

KM
0.0   2.0   4.0   6.0   8.0   10.0   12.0   14.0   16.0   18.0   20.0   22.0   24.0   26.0   28.0   30.0

Route description

After a few kilometers of Zuger flatlands along the Lorze River and up a short hill, you'll be mostly riding down the Sihl River and through its forest, the Sihlwald. With six kilometers in a bike lane on the main road from kilometer 6.7 to 12.7, this cycle is not recommended for kids, because depending on the time of day, a section of that road can be quite busy with commuter traffic.

Getting from one end to the other is easy: just follow the red signs for regional cycling route #94 from Zug to Zurich.

Sihlwald

Along the way

As mentioned above, this cycle is mostly about the protected Sihlwald, which is part of the *Wildnispark* Zürich nature reserve, a collection of woodlands that makes up the largest mixed deciduous forest in the Swiss midlands. Its trails are very popular with hikers and cyclists of all kinds, thanks also to its proximity to Zurich. In summer, the cool riverbanks draw families and groups of friends out for a day's relaxation.

The forest trail at the *Wildnispark* Zürich Sihlwald visitor's center across the river (there's a small bridge) from kilometer 16.9 introduces visitors to local flora and fauna, with information panels in German and English.

Another big draw for families is the *Wildnispark* Zürich Langenberg in Langnau am Albis, home to 19 varieties of indigenous animals, including the alpine marmot, the brown bear and the dramatically horned ibex.

Zurich

The cities of Zug and Zurich offer pretty much anything you want in terms of food. Zurich especially has one of the broadest offerings of international cuisine in Switzerland, from street vendors to fine dining. Many cafés have outdoor seating for people-watching. Parks and informal picnic spots abound along the whole route and cluster around the north end of Lake Zurich.

Public fire pits of all sizes and kinds – grated, stone-rimmed – line the Sihl River. A selection can be found at kilometers 13.5 and 15.9. The Sihlwald visitor's center (kilometer 16.9) has fire pits, picnic tables and a playground, including the forest trail mentioned above. The fire pits continue at kilometers 17.9 and 23.5. You'll notice that people will collect stones from the river to make impromptu fire pits. These are generally allowed, but before you do such a thing yourself, please read the chapter on Making Fires in Switzerland.

As part of its continued effort to completely spoil its citizens, the city of Zurich has provided a gas-powered griddle for free public use in summer. It's located by the lake across from the Blatterweise in Zürichhorn Park (search keywords "Elektrogrill Zürichhorn").

Bärlauch has so many different names in English, including wild garlic, ramsons and bear's garlic, that I'm including its Latin name: *allium ursinum*. In late winter/early spring, the Sihlwald's otherwise still mainly barren hillsides are green with this strongly flavored herb, which is used locally to spice up sausages or make pesto. While picking the plant is permitted and widely done, its resemblance to things like lily of the valley – poisonous to humans – means you should either make sure you're picking the right thing or take along an expert.

Restaurant specialties to order in Zurich include *Zürcher Geschnetzeltes* (sliced veal in mushroom cream sauce), and *Wiedikerli* sausages – which you can also buy to take home from in local butcher shops. In addition to the chocolates you already have on your list, if they are new to you try the *Luxemburgerli* (light macarons) at Confiserie Sprüngli.

Zurich

Dammed in the 1930s to generate electricity, today's shallow, slow-flowing Sihl River is hardly recognizable as the "maelstrom of the raging Sihl" from which a character is saved from drowning in 19th-century Swiss author Conrad Ferdinand Meyer's *Jürg Jenatsch*. These days, if the engineers upstream haven't open the dam a bit to regulate reservoir levels, there's just enough water for wading. Or stretching out next to for an informal barbecue, thanks also to the shade provided by the Sihlwald forest. Although an eye should be kept on food at all times, because it's also a popular place to unleash dogs, who have been known to swoop in and snag a sausage or two off a plate as they race by.

At the end of the route, Lake Zurich offers swimming all around its northern basin, in fee-based *Badis* like Mythenquai and Tiefenbrunnen (lawns, shades trees, swim rafts, piers, diving towers, slides, wading pools), and for free from the sprawling lawns of Zürihorn Park (lawns, shades trees, piers, playground with shade and water features), for example.

There's a hotel category for every taste in Zug and Zurich, as well as camping in Sihlwald.

SARGANS– ST. MARGRETHEN

Just along the Rhine

ST. GALLEN

 START
Sargans

SIGHTS
Rhine, bunkers, Liechtenstein

 FINISH
St. Margrethen

FOOD
cafés and restaurants
in towns only, picnic areas

 DISTANCE
56.01 km

SPECIALTIES
Honey, asparagus, non-alcoholic
cider, Törgga bread, Rheintaler
Ribelmais AOP

 ELEVATION GAIN
-79 m

 ASCENT
111 m

 DESCENT
190 m

SWIMMING
Rhine, Strandbad und Camping
Bruggerhorn

 KID- FRIENDLY
technically yes,
although the straight,
long ride can be
boring for them

HOTELS
mid-range, historical hotels,
B&Bs and campgrounds, premium
and luxury properties in Vaduz,
Liechtenstein

 TOURISM
tourismus.li

st.gallen-
bodensee.ch

GPX TRACK
Flat Switzerland 24

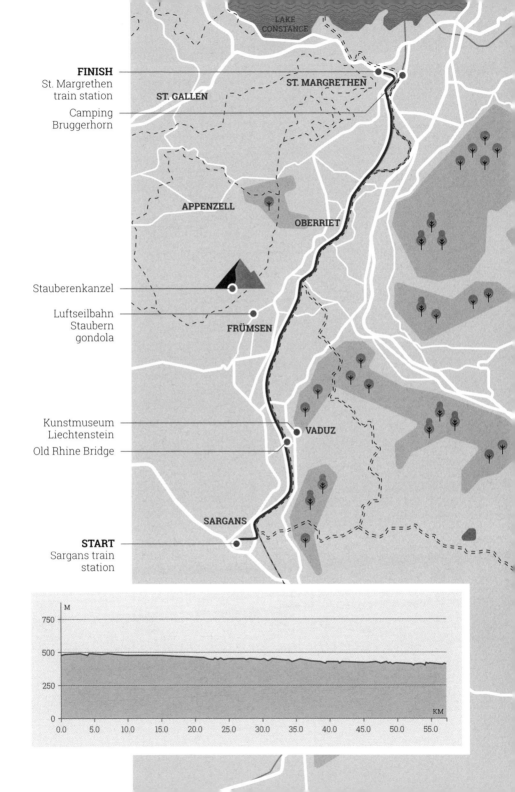

FINISH
St. Margrethen
train station

Camping
Bruggerhorn

Stauberenkanzel

Luftseilbahn
Staubern
gondola

Kunstmuseum
Liechtenstein

Old Rhine Bridge

START
Sargans train
station

LAKE
CONSTANCE

ST. MARGRETHEN

ST. GALLEN

APPENZELL

OBERRIET

FRÜMSEN

VADUZ

SARGANS

M
750
500
250
0
0.0   5.0   10.0   15.0   20.0   25.0   30.0   35.0   40.0   45.0   50.0   55.0
KM

Route description

Far from the dangerous rocks where Lorelei lures sailors to their death in southern Germany, the Rhine here is relatively calm and shallow as it winds its way slowly to Basel. The towering mountains on either side look quiet, but they hide the western highlands of Austria to the right and the popular Appenzell tourist destination to the left.

Another easy one: follow the red signs for national cycling route #2 from Sargans to St. Margrethen. You'll be riding along a raised dike next to the river.

While adults will enjoy the easy drift through the beautiful, green countryside, after an exciting look at the outside of a small bunker 20 minutes in, many kids might wonder why nothing else is happening and become bored by the long ride. If you need to abort, at kilometer 36.2 you can take the bridge over the freeway and catch route #9 into Oberriet, where there are trains to Sargans, St. Margrethen or St. Gallen.

Weite

Along the way

One of the first things you may see on your way from Sargans to the Rhine is an odd little concrete structure tucked into the foliage at kilometer 1.7. What looks like a run-down hobbit house is actually a WWII infantry bunker that used to house a large-scale machine gun as part of Switzerland's military defense system. Nineteen of these were spread across the valley and many are still visible.

If you want to add another country to your "been there" list, bring along your passport and hop over to Liechtenstein, a principality since 1719. Take the covered wooden bridge at kilometer 14.2. If the guards at the border crossing are busy, you can get your passport stamped at the tourist office. Liechtenstein's cuisine is heavily influenced by its neighbors. Where it stands out is in quality, with a whopping four restaurants with Gault Millau points within this tiny country of a mere 160 square kilometers. The spiffy town center includes the Kunstmuseum Liechtenstein, which specializes in modern art. Schloss Vaduz castle up on the hill is not open to the public; it's the prince's official residence and therefore off limits to mere mortals.

For an extraordinary view over the valley, add a side trip to the west from kilometer 26 over to the wonderfully named Frümsen. The Luftseilbahn Staubern gondola will take you up to the steep Stauberenkanzel ridge at elevation 1746 m. Once you've had your fill gawping at Liechtenstein and Austria in the distance, turn around and let the Alpstein mountains – including Mount Säntis – bowl you over. Luckily, there are avalanche barriers fixed into the hillside to stop your fall.

It's best to organize a picnic and enough to drink for this cycle. While the cafés and restaurants in Sargans and St. Margrethen are on the route, other towns are off-piste, necessitating a side trip. If you forgot something, at kilometer 15.9 there is a back gate off the cycling path to the freeway rest area, which has a restaurant and a gas station store. Official picnic sites with benches are few and far between, but you've got a 50-km stretch of riverbank to find just the right spot.

The Rhine Valley specializes in honey, asparagus, non-alcoholic cider and Rheintaler Ribelmais AOP – an exceptional cornmeal used to make the local *Törgga*, a dense bread that is also half wheat flour and spiked with raisins.

Haag

Diepoldsau

Wild swimming in the Rhine is easy here, thanks to the many access lanes that run down to the river from the raised cycling path. Keep in mind, though, that depending on the time of year, the water may be cool and the current strong.

The Strandbad und Camping Bruggerhorn outside St. Margrethen at kilometer 55.8 has its own small private lake half surrounded by lawns, with a diving tower and piers. There's also a pool – more for splashing around than swimming – with a slide, water features and a division between areas for adults and children. The littlest ones get their own separate wading pool with a fountain. The swimming area is attached to a campground.

Hotels in the valley are in the mid-range and/or historical, with premium and luxury properties in Vaduz, Liechtenstein. You'll also find B&Bs and campgrounds throughout the region.

RORSCHACH–KREUZLINGEN

Green shores of Lake Constance

SIGHTS Arbon old town, Romanshorn ferry to Friedrichshafen and Zeppelin Museum, Constance

START
Rorschach

FINISH
Kreuzlingen

FOOD cafés, restaurants, fire pits, picnic areas

DISTANCE
38.65 km

ELEVATION GAIN
2 m

SPECIALTIES apricots, plums, cherries, pears, apples and their distillations

ASCENT
207 m

DESCENT
205 m

SWIMMING Strandbad Rohrschach, Schwimmbad Badhütte Rorschach, Strandbad Arbon, Seebad Romanshorn, Schwimmbad Hörnli Kreuzlingen

KID-FRIENDLY
yes

TOURISM
thurgau-bodensee.ch

HOTELS mid-range, historical hotels and B&Bs, camping

GPX TRACK
Flat Switzerland 25

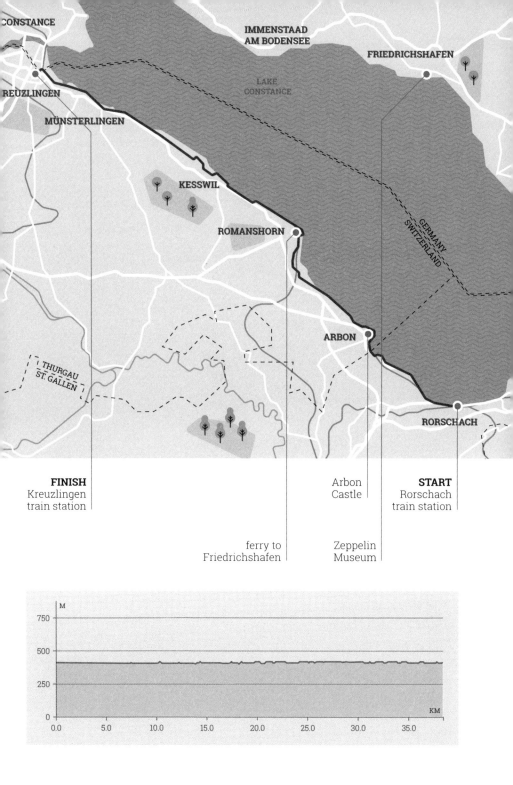

CONSTANCE

IMMENSTAAD
AM BODENSEE

FRIEDRICHSHAFEN

REUZLINGEN

LAKE
CONSTANCE

MÜNSTERLINGEN

KESSWIL

ROMANSHORN

GERMANY
SWITZERLAND

ARBON

THURGAU
ST. GALLEN

RORSCHACH

FINISH
Kreuzlingen
train station

Arbon
Castle

START
Rorschach
train station

ferry to
Friedrichshafen

Zeppelin
Museum

M

750

500

250

0

0.0   5.0   10.0   15.0   20.0   25.0   30.0   35.0

KM

Route description

Canton Thurgau's Lake Constance region is a big draw for visitors from all around – for summer vacations with swimming and camping, for cycling tours that sometimes go all the way to Basel. You won't be alone on this route.

Follow the red signs for national cycling route #2 from Rorschach to Kreuzlingen.

Along the way

The main sight here is Lake Constance – or the Bodensee, as it is called in German. As days get warmer, it becomes filled with boats, swimmers, pedalos and SUPs, as people picnic and relax on the lawns along its shores.

If you're in the mood to stroll through medieval old towns, start with Arbon. It's very small, but a closer look reveals its origins as Arbor Felix, a Roman town on the northwestern border of the Imperial Province of Rhaetia. The Museum in Arbon Castle has a historical exhibition with Roman artifacts found in the region.

Romanshorn

From Romanshorn, a ferry takes you to Friedrichshafen (in Germany, bring your passport). The Zeppelin Museum there includes a replica of an airship passenger cabin that you can walk around in.

In Kreuzlingen, you can cross the border into Constance by continuing along Wiesenstrasse at kilometer 37.7. Border checks are infrequent, but make sure to carry a passport here as well. Constance's old town is a popular shopping destination, with a wide variety of places to lunch in, and its harborside Stadtpark promenade draws crowds on sunny days.

Arbon

There are plenty of waterfront cafés, restaurants and picnic areas along this lake-focused cycle. Rorschach, Arbon, Romanshorn and Kreuzlingen have the largest supermarkets. There are several grated fire pits on the route, such as just 100 m from Rorschach's train station, at kilometer 5.6 in the harbor park in Steinach, kilometer 8.9 in the lakeside park in Arbon, kilometer 17 out on the harbor point in Romanshorn and kilometer 23.8 outside Kesswil.

Another one of Switzerland's fruit baskets, Canton Thurgau is known especially for its apples. For local fruit in season, go in summer to be on time for fresh apricots, plums, cherries and pears, too. Dried apple rings are a traditional edible souvenir. Farmers let their imaginations run free, finding new markets for their harvests by turning them into products like apricot mustard and liquors of all kinds – "barrique golden delicious" apple brandy or hay schnaps, for example.

There are many free parks along Lake Constance to swim from, which makes it a great place for spontaneity. If you're ready for a *Badi* right off the train, Strandbad Rohrschach (3 pools including lengths and wading, lawns, shade trees, lake access) is right there for you. A few hundred meters further on, Schwimmbad Badhütte Rorschach is a historic bathhouse on stilts in the lake accessed by a pedestrian bridge from the lakeshore. Its quadrangle shape forms a sheltered pool and on its outer terrace a few metal steps down or a jump from the diving board take you out to the swim rafts on the lake. Other fee-based *Badis* include Strandbad Arbon (bathing, lengths, large slide and 10-meter diving tower, wading, lawns and shade trees, lake access), Seebad Romanshorn (bathing, lengths, slide, counter-current pool, diving towers, wading, lawns and shade trees, lake access) and Schwimmbad Hörnli Kreuzlingen (bathing, lengths, diving, wading, slides, playgrounds, lawns and shade trees, beach).

You'll find accommodations in the mid-range, in addition to historical hotels, B&Bs and camping throughout this route. The lovely medieval town of Gottlieben, just 2 km west of Kreuzlingen, has a few charming premium hotels right on the Rhine.

Kreuzlingen

KREUZLINGEN– STEIN AM RHEIN

Down the lazy Rhine between medieval towns

THURGAU, SCHAFFHAUSEN

SIGHTS

Gottlieben, Arenenberg Castle, Stein am Rhein

 START

Kreuzlingen

 FINISH

Stein am Rhein

FOOD

cafés, restaurants, fire pits, picnic areas

 DISTANCE

30.43 km

ELEVATION GAIN

10 m

SPECIALTIES

Gottlieber Hüppen wafer rolls filled with chocolate, *Wiigueteli* cookie spices, Swiss souvenirs, Pinot Noir

▲ **ASCENT**

231 m

▼ **DESCENT**

221 m

SWIMMING

Strandbad Rohrschach, Schwimmbad Badhütte Rorschach, Strandbad Buchhorn Arbon, Seebad Romanshorn, Schwimmbad Hörnli Kreuzlingen

 KID-FRIENDLY

yes

TOURISM

thurgau-bodensee.ch

tourismus.steinamrhein.ch

HOTELS

mid-range, historical hotels and B&Bs, camping, boutique hotels in Gottlieben

 GPX TRACK

Flat Switzerland 26

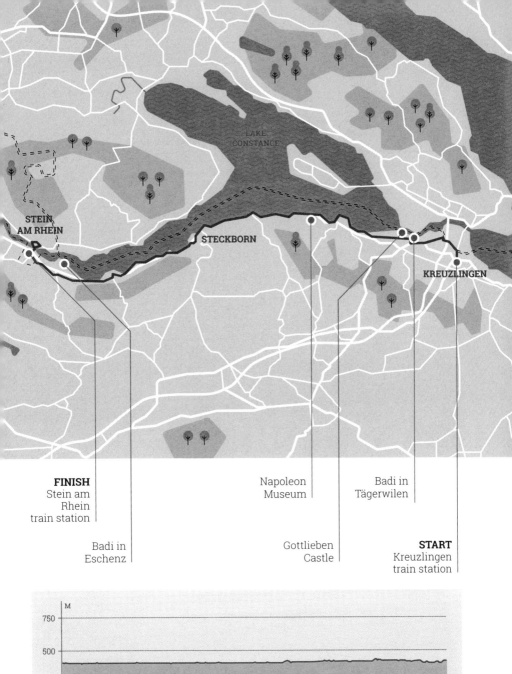

LAKE
CONSTANCE

STEIN
AM RHEIN

STECKBORN

KREUZLINGEN

FINISH
Stein am
Rhein
train station

Badi in
Eschenz

Napoleon
Museum

Gottlieben
Castle

Badi in
Tägerwilen

START
Kreuzlingen
train station

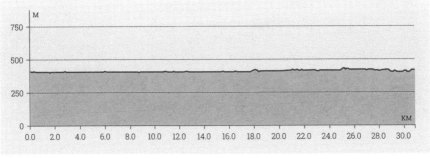

Route description

This region of "Lower Lake Constance" (Untersee) is quieter and has simpler *Badis* (often just a small lawn and lake access, but also mostly free) than its eastern neighbor (see Flat Switzerland 25). With the charming towns of Gottlieben and Stein am Rhein on either end, it is a great route for fans of the medieval Swiss experience.

Follow the red signs for national cycling route #2 from Kreuzlingen to Stein am Rhein. Although you are allowed to cycle through the latter's main street, the many pedestrians have the right of way, so as the signs say: "*Bitte im Schritttempo*" – please cycle at walking speed. Better yet, get off and push or lock it up nearby.

Along the way

A day-out destination for both tourists and locals, Gottlieben is dominated by half-timbered houses, some dating back to the 13th century, and a waterfront promenade lined with hotels, cafés and restaurants. The Hotel Drachenburg, with its impressive 19th-century metal dragon projecting from the façade, is an attraction reminiscent of a time when the town was a stop for royal visits. The town's castle is privately owned, so it can only be admired from the outside.

History buffs and fans of 19th-century interior design should check out the Napoleon Museum in Arenenberg Castle up the hill in Salenstein. It was home to Hortense de Beauharnais, Queen consort of Holland, and her son Charles Louis Napoléon Bonaparte, the future Napoleon III and nephew of the original. The art, furnishings and gardens of the property are a great example of the period's opulence.

Stein am Rhein is best known for the luxuriously painted facades on its townhouses, especially along its main street, Unterstadt. Its well-maintained medieval old town is exemplary – mentally add some grime and the right smells and you can imagine yourself in historical Switzerland. Brace yourself for a crowd: it's a popular stop for bus tours and Rhine cruise ships.

Cafés and restaurants that are open all day mainly cluster around Kreuzlingen, Gottlieben and Stein am Rhein. You'll find large supermarkets for picnic supplies in Kreuzlingen and Stein am Rhein. There are grated fire pits at kilometer 3.2 (part of the free *Badi* in Tägerwilen, see below), kilometers 6.85, 11.6 (stay on the lake side of the tracks for 20 meters) and 25.3 (turn right towards the lake and down to the free *Badi* in Eschenz, which also has a few picnic tables). There are many bench opportunities for a picturesque picnic throughout this route.

If you're looking for edible souvenirs to take home, you'll need to stop almost before you've started: *Gottlieber Hüppen* wafer rolls filled with chocolate are the specialty of the town of Gottlieben – which is very much worth a visit anyway (see above). Look for *Wiigueteli* cookie spices, an essential addition to cookies made with red wine, in Stein am Rhein. This is also where you'll find bells, watches, pocketknives and other traditionally Swiss souvenirs. When you're done, rest on the town's Rhine promenade with a glass of local Pinot Noir.

There are many *Badis* with Rhine access on this route. They include Seerheinbad Zellersguet Tägerwilen (swim rafts, diving tower, lawns, shade trees, playground, grated fire pits), Strandbad Salenstein (basic lawn with swim raft), Badi Mannenbach (lawn, playground, showers, fire pit), Strandbad Steckborn (swim rafts, diving tower, large wading pool, lawns, pier, playground, campground next door), Strandbad Eschenz a.k.a *Buebebadi* (lawns, a few shade trees, playground, bathrooms, changing rooms).

The Schwimmbad Espi in Stein am Rhein charges minimal admission for its fenced-in bathing area (no swimming), manicured lawn, playground with slide (not water), changing rooms, bathrooms, showers. A kiosk sells homemade snacks and has tables with parasols.

Most of this region offers mid-range, historical hotels and B&Bs, with campgrounds here and there. Gottlieben's historical old town is perfect for an overnight at the beginning of this route, also thanks to a few boutique hotels.

Stein
am Rhein

STEIN–BASEL

Historical bridges, power stations and Romans

AARGAU, BASEL-
LANDSCHAFT,
GERMANY,
BASEL-STADT

 START

Stein

 FINISH

Basel

SIGHTS Roman ruins, Stein/Bad Säckingen old town, Basel old town

 DISTANCE

39.23 km

FOOD cafés, restaurants (international cuisine in Basel), fire pits, picnic areas

 ELEVATION GAIN

-21 m

SPECIALTIES Swabian *Maultaschen*, Basler Läckerli cookies, see also Flat Switzerland 28 and 29

 ASCENT

283 m

 DESCENT

304 m

SWIMMING Rhine parks, Freibad Bachtalen, KuBa in Rheinfelden

 KID-FRIENDLY

yes

 TOURISM

basel.ch

augustaraurica.ch

badsaeckingen.de

HOTELS mid-range, historical hotels and B&Bs, camping, all ranges in Basel

 GPX TRACK

Flat Switzerland 27

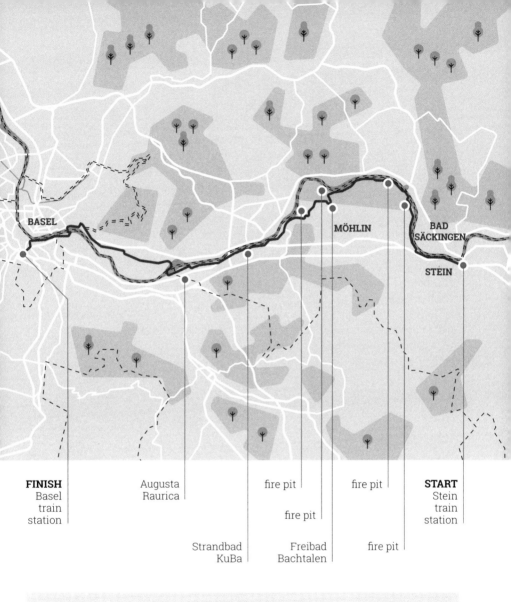

FINISH
Basel
train
station

Augusta
Raurica

fire pit

fire pit

START
Stein
train
station

fire pit

fire pit

Strandbad
KuBa

Freibad
Bachtalen

fire pit

BASEL

MÖHLIN

BAD
SÄCKINGEN

STEIN

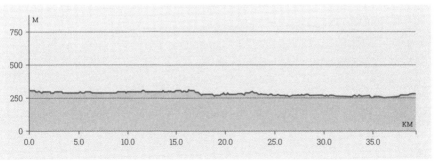

Route description

If you are interested in Roman history – or are looking to offer your kids a Roman adventure – this is the cycle for you. Or ignore the Romans and just enjoy a peaceful zip along the Rhine to Basel, through forests, fields and over one of the river's most imposing hydroelectric power stations.

From the train station in Stein, follow the red signs for national cycling route #2 to the Staustufe Augst/Wyhlen power station in Kaiseraugst. Cross its dam to Germany (the signs tell you to get off and walk) and at the other end (kilometer 27) pick up the *15 EuroVelo Rheinradweg* bike path to Basel.

Bring your passport or ID card for the crossing to and from Germany. Although there are seldom border checks, it's good to be prepared.

Along the way

While Stein as a whole is not a tourist destination, its 16th-century wooden bridge over to Bad Säckingen in Germany definitely is. The old town of Bad Säckingen draws both Swiss and Germans for day trips, thanks to its strollable streets, baroque church and many shops.

The ruins of Roman watchtowers and a *castel* outside of Stein in the Riburg Forest conjure up the 4th-century Roman Empire, when the Rhine formed a northern border and soldiers were positioned here to keep an eye on restless Alemanni, who had their eye on Roman lands. About 12 kilometers down the cycling path and up the hill in Kaiseraugst, Augusta Raurica is a huge archeological site that has been turned into an open-air museum. It has a replica of a Roman house and several other features that offer insight into what it was like to live in Roman times.

Basel's famous old town is always worth a wander, thanks to its Münster and the Pfalz viewpoint, the stunning red façade of its city hall with a fresh produce market (weekdays) in front. Give yourself time to meander through its narrow streets: even if you've been here before, you're bound to make a delightful discovery just around the next corner.

Food served by others gets increasingly frequent as you move closer towards Basel. There are some cafés and restaurants in Stein (and especially Bad Säckingen, if you are doing that side trip), otherwise hold out for Basel, where the options range from food stall to linen tablecloths and the cuisine is international.

Or plan on a picnic (supermarkets are available all along the way). There are a series of grated fire pits in the Riburg Forest at kilometers 6.3, 8.5 (both close to the ruins of Roman watchtowers), 12.5 (by the ruins of a Roman *castel*, see above), 13.8 (turn right onto Kraftwerkstrasse and take it to the picnic area with two large fire pits and shade trees next to the Kraftwerk Riburg power station) and 16.

The old town Bad Säckingen in Germany is geared towards tourists, with quite a few Mediterranean specialty shops (oil, truffles, spices), but you'll find the famous Swabian *Maultaschen* here. These are a kind of large meat-filled dumpling similar to ravioli, but about four times the size, and usually filled with minced and smoked meat, spinach, breadcrumbs and onions.

Since this is the first of three chapters to include Basel, for food souvenirs from Switzerland's third-largest city let's start with *Basler-Läckerli*, the famous Swiss gingerbread cousin made with nuts, honey, oranges and lemons. Please see also Flat Switzerland 28 and 29 for more *Basler* specialty options.

Staustufe Augst/ Wyhlen power station

Basel

There are small parks all along this route that you can swim from, but be aware that this section of the Rhine is subject to changing water levels and currents. Please always pay attention to warning signs and swim at your own risk!

Badis on land that charge admission include Freibad Bachtalen in Möhlin with 4 pools (bathing, lengths, diving, wading) and slide, lawns and shade trees, as well as Strandbad KuBa in Rheinfelden with 2 pools (bathing, lengths), 2 slides, lawns, shade trees and access to enclosed river section with diving boards.

As with cafes and restaurants, the variety of hotels increases the closer you get to Basel, with mid-range and historical hotels, B&Bs and camping beforehand and all ranges in Basel.

BASEL CIRCLE

3 countries and a Rhine float

BASEL-STADT,
GERMANY,
FRANCE

 START

Basel

SIGHTS

Kunstmuseum Basel, Fondation Beyeler, Museum Tinguely, Vitra Museum

 FINISH

Basel

FOOD

cafés, restaurants (international cuisine), fire pit, picnic areas

 DISTANCE

32.48 km

SPECIALTIES

Uussteller sausage, *Anisbrot* anise cookie, *Magenbrot* gingerbread with chocolate, *Mässmogge* candies, see also Flat Switzerland 27 and 29

 ELEVATION GAIN

0 m

 ASCENT

182 m

SWIMMING

Rhine, Laguna Badeland in Weil, Parc des Eaux Vives in Huningue (watersports only, no actual swimming)

 DESCENT

182 m

 KID-FRIENDLY

yes

 TOURISM

basel.ch
ville-huningue.fr
weil-am-rhein.de

HOTELS

all ranges in Basel

 GPX TRACK

Flat Switzerland 28

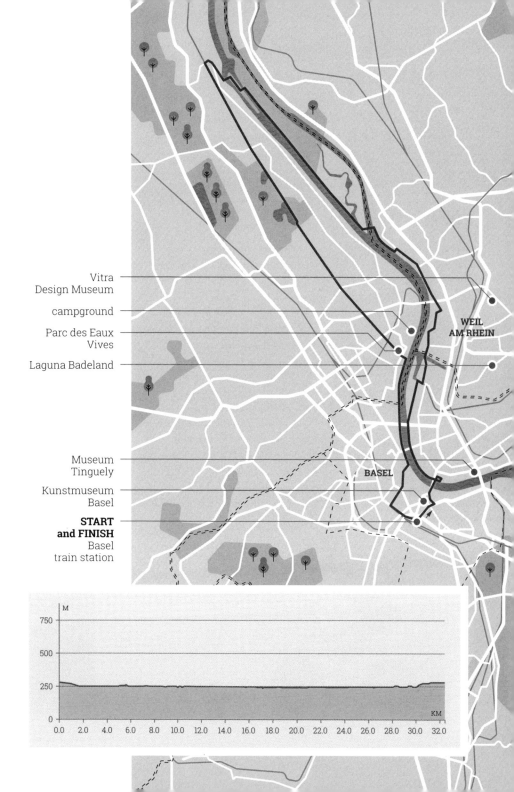

Vitra
Design Museum
campground
Parc des Eaux
Vives
Laguna Badeland

WEIL
AM RHEIN

Museum
Tinguely
Kunstmuseum
Basel

BASEL

**START
and FINISH**
Basel
train station

M
750
500
250
0

KM

0.0 2.0 4.0 6.0 8.0 10.0 12.0 14.0 16.0 18.0 20.0 22.0 24.0 26.0 28.0 30.0 32.0

Route description

This international cycle takes you through three countries – Switzerland, Germany, France – and surroundings that change from city center to industry, riverside, countryside and back again. It's a great way to get a look at the scope of a major Rhine harbor. Bring your passport or ID card. Although there are seldom border checks, keep an eye out for the border police when you cross.

In front of the Basel SBB train station, take one of the bike ramps to your left or right that go underneath the square. They take you through the underground bicycle parking garage to the Aeschengraben bike lane next to De-Wette Park. Follow that to Aeschenplatz, where you turn left onto Brunngässlein, which joins Dufourstrasse. Turn right onto St. Alban-Graben, where you join national cycling route #2. Take this all the way to the German border in Weil am Rhein. Once in Germany, follow Zollstrasse, which turns into Colmarer Strasse (the cycling path is safely on the sidewalk) and turn left onto Alte Strasse. At kilometer 9.3, turn left onto the side street (also called Alte Strasse; there's a sign for the Gasthaus am Bootssteg). Turn right at the river and go along the cycling path for 900 meters and turn left onto the bridge onto the Ile du Rhin, where you join cycling route #979. Follow that all the way back to Basel and route #7 at kilometer 30. That takes you back to the Basel SBB train station.

Weil am Rhein

Along the way

With almost 40 museums and many galleries, Basel is arguably Switzerland's top spot for art. Not to be missed are the central Kunstmuseum Basel and the Museum Tinguely, the Fondation Beyeler in nearby Riehen, and the Vitra Design Museum in Weil am Rhein, Germany. The buildings themselves are a draw for fans of modern architecture.

Basel has all the stores you need to put together a picnic. There's a fire pit off kilometer 24.5 in France: turn left onto the bridge that takes you onto Rue du Général de Gaulle and through Village-Neuf, turn left onto Boulevard d'Alsace and right onto the small Rue du Rhin. The picnic area is to the left at the river's edge. There are some riverside restaurants and benches everywhere along the Rhine in Germany and France, and of course Basel offers all price ranges in international cuisine.

Barrage de Kembs

Basel is rich with culinary specialties. Look for *Uussteller*, a finely ground beef, veal and pork sausage, *Anisbrot* anise cookies, *Magenbrot*, a kind of gingerbread made with chocolate, and *Mässmogge*, thumb-sized flavored candies with hazelnut filling (see also Flat Switzerland 27 and 29).

Il du Rhin

There's a full-on aquatic center in Weil am Rhein, the Laguna Badeland. At kilometer 5, turn right onto Neuhausenstrasse to the German border crossing, then straight ahead along bike path to Nonnenholzstrasse and through the forest to the center's entrance. It has five pools (different temperatures, diving, wading, water features, outdoor, lengths, slide, waves).

The Parc des Eaux Vives on the Canal de Huningue in France has an outdoor whitewater canal with fountains and playgrounds for the kids, and climbing walls and rentals (kayaks, rafts, riverboards, SUP) for teenagers and adults.

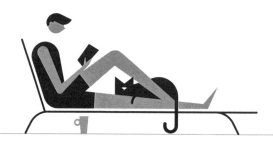

In general, swim in the Rhine at your own risk. Due to the significant danger posed by currents, eddies and large ships transporting goods to and from Rotterdam, swimming is not allowed in much of the Rhine from Basel's harbor downstream to France. Look for signs where swimming is permitted.

In Kleinbasel, good swimmers may enter the Rhine from the riverbank just below the Museum Tinguely at Paul Sacher-Anlage 1. From there you can float or swim down the Rhine along the Kleinbasel side. Get yourself a *Wickelfisch* – an airtight floating bag for your clothes – from a local store and you're all set for some water-based sightseeing.

Every August, the SLRG Swiss lifeguard association organizes a one-day supervised swim that draws thousands of locals and tourists.

Some don'ts from Basel's police: You may not swim with inflatable flotation devices (air mattresses, bathing rings) of any kind. You may not swim out into the shipping lane in the middle of the river or cross over to Grossbasel – stay inside the swim channel buoys on the Kleinbasel side. You must leave the river at the very latest 200 meters before Dreirosenbrücke, where the end of Offenburgerstrasse meets Unterer Rheinweg. There are stairs to get out, as well as showers and bathrooms, all along the Kleinbasel riverbank.

Have a post-swim drink or meal at one of the many *buvettes* – snack stands with seating – on the banks of the river in Kleinbasel.

Basel is your best bet for overnights, with all hotel ranges and styles on offer. St. Louis in France and Weil am Rhein in Germany tend to be a bit cheaper, with mid-range hotels. There is a campground in France before the Passerelle des Trois Pays.

Huningue

BASEL– FRANCE–BASEL

From town to fields to quiet forest

BASEL-STADT, BASEL-LANDSCHAFT, FRANCE

SIGHTS Ruine Landskron, modern Basel architecture and street art

FOOD cafés, restaurants (international cuisine), picnic spots

SPECIALTIES *Eierkirsch* liqueur, *Cenovis* sandwich spread, *Pepita* grapefruit soda, see also Flat Switzerland 27 and 28

SWIMMING Rhine, Gartenbad Bottmingen

HOTELS mid-range, historical hotels and B&Bs, Basel all ranges

 START
Basel

 FINISH
Basel

 DISTANCE
36.30 km

 ELEVATION GAIN
0 m

 ASCENT
386 m

 DESCENT
386 m

 KID-FRIENDLY
yes

 TOURISM
basel.ch

GPX TRACK
Flat Switzerland 29

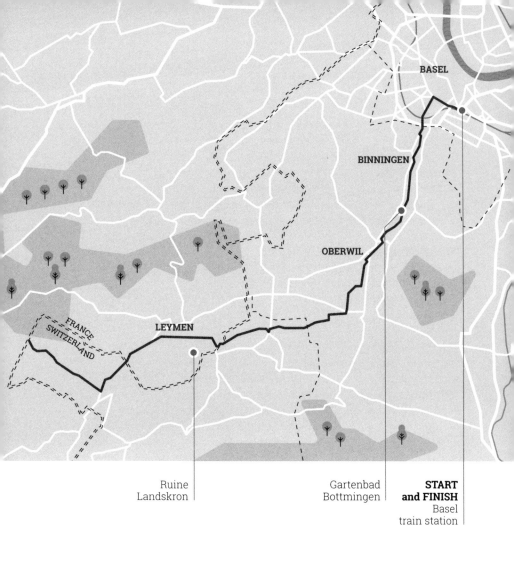

BASEL

BINNINGEN

OBERWIL

FRANCE
SWITZERLAND

LEYMEN

Ruine
Landskron

Gartenbad
Bottmingen

**START
and FINISH**
Basel
train station

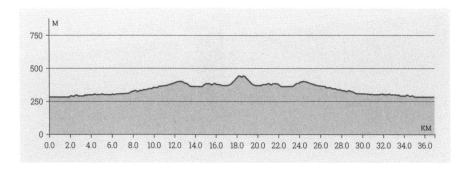

M

750

500

250

0

KM

0.0 2.0 4.0 6.0 8.0 10.0 12.0 14.0 16.0 18.0 20.0 22.0 24.0 26.0 28.0 30.0 32.0 34.0 36.0

Route description

From Basel's busy center, take a relaxing ride out through the suburbs and into the quiet countryside and back to the city again. This route briefly goes through France – although you may not even notice you've changed countries. And once you're in Switzerland again, you may not be where you think you should be. I expected the end of the way out to be in Basel-Landschaft, but instead found myself in Solothurn. A quick search for "map of Switzerland with cantons" told me that Solothurn does indeed have an exclave on the French border. In any case, bring your passport or ID card. While there are no manned border crossings, you'll still technically be in another country for 3.3 km each way.

Take national cycling route #7 from the Basel SBB train station to kilometer 13.3, where you switch to #97, go through France for a bit and arrive in Rodersdorf (Solothurn). There, at kilometer 16, route #97 is also signposted as the Dreiland-Radweg towards Mulhouse. After another 2.5 km, you'll be in the forest at the French border, where you'll turn around and head back to Basel.

Binningen

Along the way

History buffs and fans of crumbling castles are encouraged to go up the steep hill to the Ruine Landskron above Leymen in France. It dates back to 1297 and was destroyed in 1813, but a French-Swiss non-profit has been slowly restoring it since the end of the last century. It offers a gorgeous view of the Alsace, the Vosges Mountains, the Black Forest and the Rhine plain.

While better-known for its superb medieval old town, Basel's modern side also deserves a closer look. Award-winning, internationally active architects have designed exceptional buildings here that include the Zentralstellwerk SBB railway control tower and the Stadtcasino (Herzog & De Meuron), the Kunstmuseum Basel Neubau (Christ & Gantenbein), the Fondation Beyeler museum in nearby Riehen (Renzo Piano) and the Museum Tinguely (Mario Botta).

And while you're cycling from one to the other, keep an eye out for Basel's vibrant street art. It flourishes at commissioned sites like the mural of rock musicians at Gerbergässlein and the ever-changing elaborate pieces of the Sommercasino at Münchensteinerstrasse 1. Of course there are also wilder variants that spring up organically on "unofficial" walls throughout the city – some as brilliant as anything found in an art gallery.

There are plenty of cafés and restaurants along this route, with the most selection and international cuisine in Basel, as you'd expect. Spontaneous picnic spots are easy to come by from about kilometer 8 onwards, and you'll find numerous supermarkets on your way there.

Continuing the list from Flat Switzerland 27 and 28, the Basler countryside surrounding the city has innovated specialties like *Eierkirsch*, (a very sweet liqueur made with eggs, *Kirsch*, cream and vanilla), *Cenovis* (a Swiss cousin to Vegemite and Marmite), and my favorite, *Pepita* grapefruit soda from Eptingen.

If you're ready for a swim, Gartenbad Bottmingen charges admission for its three pools (lengths, diving, bathing with slide) and has lawns, shade trees, a small wading pool with shade and a playground for the kiddies. And yes, that is a castle next door. There are no tours, unfortunately, but Schloss Bottmingen does house a high-tone restaurant with an outdoor garden terrace.

The Rhine can be dangerous in places, so please read the extensive section on swimming in the river in Flat Switzerland 28. The Birsig is not for swimming.

Hotels out in the countryside tend to be mid-range or historical, with some B&Bs. The city of Basel has everything from stripped down budget hotels to luxurious, "Queen Elizabeth II slept here" riverfront properties with all frills intact.

BERN–NEUCHÂTEL

From old Bern to the flatlands
of Lake Neuchâtel

BERN,
FRIBOURG,
NEUCHÂTEL

 START

Bern

 FINISH

Bern old town, Neuchâtel old
town and castle

Neuchâtel

 DISTANCE

53.31 km

cafés, restaurants
(international cuisine),
fire pits, picnic areas

 **ELEVATION
GAIN**

-63 m

 ASCENT

489 m

Ovomaltine/Ovaltine, Ragusa and
Toblerone chocolate, *Mandelbärli*
and *Kambly Bretzeli* cookies,
Swiss Highland Whisky, *Ingwerer*
ginger liqueur, see also Flat
Switzerland 7, 8 and 31

 DESCENT

552 m

 **KID–
FRIENDLY**

yes, take the
funicular up to
Neuchâtel's train
station at the end

Aare, Freibad Marzili,
Lake Neuchâtel

 TOURISM

bern.com

j3l.ch

Bern all ranges, business hotels,
camping, stylish boutiques in
Neuchatel

 GPX TRACK

Flat Switzerland 30

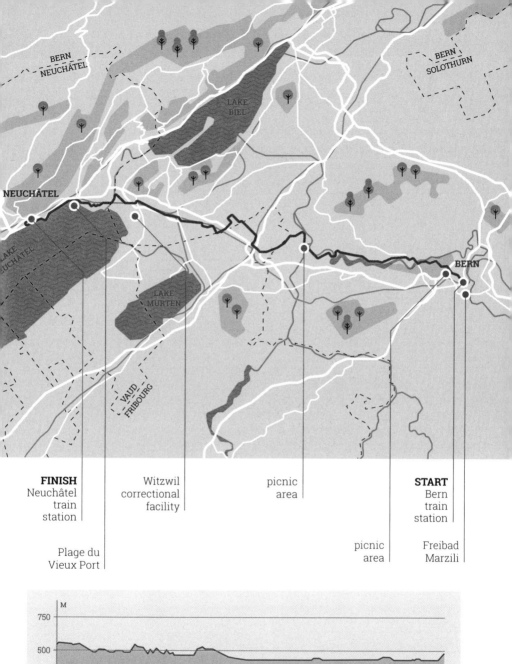

FINISH	Witzwil	picnic	START
Neuchâtel	correctional	area	Bern
train	facility		train
station			station

		picnic	Freibad
Plage du		area	Marzili
Vieux Port			

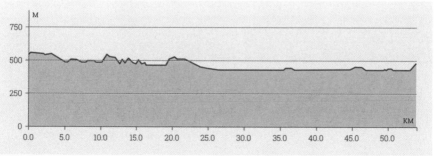

Route description

It's a quick ride out of Bern from the train station: you'll be in the forest and on your way to Neuchâtel after less than two kilometers. After a peaceful cycle along the Wohlen reservoir, past a power station and through the village of Kerzers, you'll be on the flatlands of the Grosses Moos or Great Marsh, one of Switzerland's important agricultural regions.

You won't have to worry much about directions: just follow regional cycling route #94 from Bern to Neuchâtel. There you can either go up the steep hill to the train station, or at kilometer 51.4 turn right onto Rue Coulon to Avenue du Premier-Mars, cross that and take the Fun'Ambule funicular up. Bicycles need their own ticket and are only allowed if there is space available, so avoid rush hour.

Hofen

Along the way

Wander from shop to shop through Bern's old town underneath its famous covered, raised sidewalks. They start on Spitalgasse by the train station and continue straight down to Gerechtigkeitsgasse (the name of the street changes names every block or so, but it's the same one all the way). You'll also pass by the Zytglogge bell tower, which is festooned with mechanical characters who put on a show once an hour.

Neuchâtel's old town at the bottom of the hill from the train station is lined with delicatessens, cheese shops and bistros that offer local dishes. Looming above, the castle that gives the city its name (and dates back to the 12th century) now houses the cantonal government.

Schürhubel
Woods

Bern is nicely sprinkled with all sorts of cafés and restaurants, some offering international cuisine. Neuchâtel is a little more locally oriented, making it a good place to try out specialties like *papet vaudois*, a stew made with sausages and leeks (see also Flat Switzerland 8).

Ready for a barbecue right away? There's a picnic area in the woods at the edge of Bern with a fire pit at kilometer 1.5. Further on, there's one at kilometer 17.8 in the little river delta, just before you cross over the trail bridge.

Canton Bern is the original source of *Ovomaltine* (or *Ovaltine* in English, thanks to a misspelling on the trademark registration), which comes in all kinds of different forms: pressed into bars, as a crunchy spread and in bags of "rocks". Other brands of chocolate that come from Bern are the *Ragusa* hazelnut bar and the world-renowned *Toblerone*, which includes the Bernese bear on its iconic packaging (as a "shadow" on the side of the Matterhorn).

Grosses
Moos

If you haven't eaten enough sweets yet, try *Mandelbärli* bear-shaped almond cookies and *Kambly Bretzeli*, wafer-thin sugar cookies with lemon. Wash them all down with a Swiss Highland Whisky or *Ingwerer* ginger liqueur (see also Flat Switzerland 7, 8 and 31).

At the foot of Switzerland's Bundeshaus parliament building, nestled into a bend in the Aare River, is Freibad Marzili. With spacious lawns and shade trees throughout its park, it has 5 pools (2 bathing, lengths, wading, diving), access to the Aare River along its 300-meter waterfront, and it's free. No wonder this is one of the most legendary *Badis* in the country.

Although not as tricky as the Rhine in Basel, you still need to be careful when you're swimming in the Aare in Bern: there's a dam just downstream from the Freibad Marzili, so swimming past the Dalmazibrücke is not permitted (look for the red and white signs).

Once you've left Bern, the next good swim stops are along Wohlensee and the Aare before Kerzers, and then after you've crossed the Grosses Moos, at Lake Neuchâtel. There are a few bays scooped out on the Plage du Vieux Port public park in Hauterive where the water is warmer. Up the lake in Neuchâtel, the Plage des Jeunes-Rives, Plage Suchard and Plage de Serrières are all free and have little beaches.

Out in the Grosses Moos between Kerzers and Neuchâtel (about 3 km southwest of kilometer 36.2), you can support the resocialization of the prisoners in the Witzwil correctional facility by shopping at their store. It's located outside the prison and sells produce grown and gifts crafted by the inmates, who are offered a chance to complete an apprenticeship in agriculture during their incarceration.

As an international capital, Bern caters to all kinds of hotel guests and budgets – including a campground just outside Bern at kilometer 5.1.

BERN–THUN

Up the emerald Aare to Lake Thun

BERN

SIGHTS Bern's Parliament Building, Thun old town and Donjon castle

FOOD cafés, restaurants (international cuisine), fire pits, picnic areas

SPECIALTIES *Belper Knolle* garlic cheese, *Blaues Hirni* fresh blue cheese; *Emmentaler AOP*, see also Flat Switzerland 30

SWIMMING Aare River, Freibad Marzili, Strandbad Eichholz, Parkbad Münsingen, Strandbad Thun

HOTELS all ranges in Bern and Thun, camping outside Bern and Thun

 START
Bern

 FINISH
Thun

 DISTANCE
33.28 km

 ELEVATION GAIN
13 m

 ASCENT
219 m

 DESCENT
206 m

 KID-FRIENDLY
yes

 TOURISM
bern.com
thunersee.ch

 GPX TRACK
Flat Switzerland 31

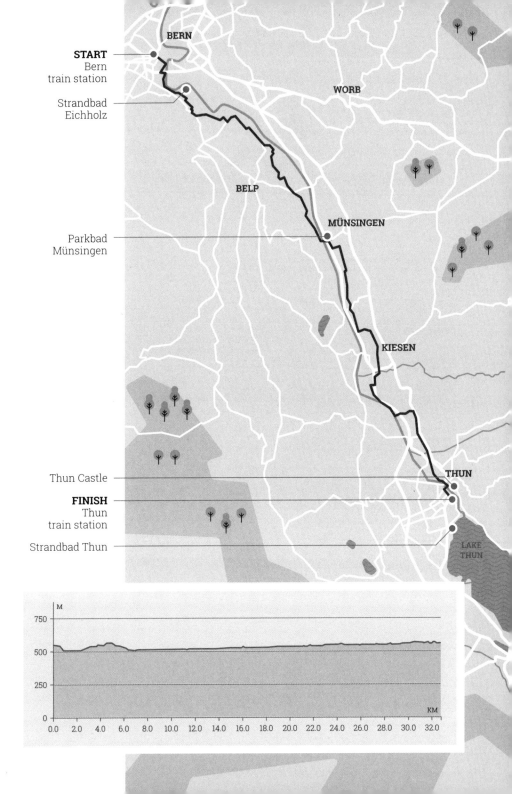

START
Bern
train station

Strandbad
Eichholz

BERN

WORB

BELP

Parkbad
Münsingen

MÜNSINGEN

KIESEN

Thun Castle

FINISH
Thun
train station

Strandbad Thun

THUN

LAKE
THUN

M
750

500

250

0

0.0   2.0   4.0   6.0   8.0   10.0   12.0   14.0   16.0   18.0   20.0   22.0   24.0   26.0   28.0   30.0   32.0

KM

Schönausteg

Route description

This cycle is dominated by the wide Aare River. In summer, you'll meet people in, around and on it as they picnic, swim and float boats down from Thun. Because it's a short route, you'll have plenty of time to do a lot of the same. Bring at least a picnic blanket and your bathing suit.

Here as well, it's hard to get lost: from Bern's train station, follow national cycling route #8 to Thun.

Along the way

Completed in 1902, the *Curia Confoederationis Helveticae* (officially the *Bundeshaus* in German and the Parliament Building in English) is the seat of the Swiss federal government. The domed entrance hall is laid out in the shape of a cross and is filled with sculptures, stained glass windows and plaster reliefs by artists from around the country. You can see it as part of a guided tour only, except on four open house days throughout the year.

Thun's old town hugs the northern tip of Lake Thun where the Aare River starts its way to Bern. It's easily strollable in a few hours, shopping included. In the Schloss Thun castle overlooking the town, the 12th-century Donjon tower houses a historical museum where you can learn all about the city and its surroundings. A hotel with restaurant and a conference center occupies part of the newer buildings. If you don't feel like walking up to the castle, there's an elevator at Obere Hauptgasse 27 that will carry you to the top.

Thun

Heimberg

As two of Switzerland's most-visited tourists destinations, both Bern and Thun have a wide range of cafés and restaurants offering international cuisine. Stock up on picnic supplies at one of the numerous supermarkets – you'll find many options for an outdoor pit stop along the route. There are several fire pits in Strandbad Eichholz (down the hill at kilometer 3.2), and another at kilometer 15.7 next to the Parkbad Münsingen, in the picnic area beside the parking lot.

Take home some of the region's most notable cheeses. None is more distinct that the *Belper Knolle*, a ball of cheese spiced with garlic or herbs that comes in either fresh or hard. The wonderfully named *Blaues Hirni* (blue brain – you'll understand why when you see one) looks awful from the outside, but the grey-blue mold hides a tasty, fresh cheese that goes great with prosecco. If you're new to the area and since you're so close, get some local Emmentaler AOP – the original Swiss cheese with the holes in it that inspired so many imitations – and discover what it's really supposed to taste like. (See also Flat Switzerland 30.)

On a bend in the Aare River, Freibad Marzili in Bern has a view of Switzerland's Parliament Building. This free *Badi* is set by the Aare River in a spacious park with shade trees. It has 5 pools (2 bathing, lengths, wading, diving) and access to the Aare River along its 300-meter waterfront. But look out for the dam just downstream; swimming past the Dalmazibrücke is not permitted.

Down the hill at kilometer 3.2 is Strandbad Eichholz, a large park popular with families and groups out for a day by the river. You can let yourself drift down to Freibad Marzili, but you'll need to walk back up from there in your bathing suit (about 20 minutes). Or see the "*Badis* and Campgrounds" chapter for floating bag solutions, so you can take your clothes with you and keep them dry.

Parks that charge admission include the Parkbad in Münsingen, which has access to the Aare plus three pools (bathing/lengths, diving, wading), lawns, shade trees and a playground.

Münsingen

The extensive Strandbad on Lake Thun has pools for lengths, bathing, diving and wading, with slides, lawns, shade trees, a playground and a beach.

Like the Rhine in Basel (see Flat Switzerland 28), the Aare in Bern has a few things you need to look out for. It's best to stick to where others are swimming and be aware of the signage: square red and white ones mean no swimming is allowed.

Accommodations in Bern and Thun include all ranges and there is camping outside Bern and Thun.

SAMEDAN CIRCLE

Basking in Engadiner light

GRAUBÜNDEN

SIGHTS
Bever, Muottas Muragl,
San Gian church, Chesa Planta

FOOD
cafés, restaurants,
picnic areas

SPECIALTIES
*Bündner Nusstorte, Engadiner
Torte, Bündnerfleisch, Capuns,
Pizokel*

SWIMMING
Mineralbad & Spa Samedan,
Lej da Staz, Ovaverva Pool
Spa & Sports Centre St. Moritz

HOTELS
all ranges, especially chalets,
historical, luxury

START
Samedan

FINISH
Samedan

DISTANCE
36.76 km

**ELEVATION
GAIN**
0 m

ASCENT
380 m

DESCENT
380 m

**KID-
FRIENDLY**
yes

TOURISM
engadin.ch

GPX TRACK
Flat Switzerland 32

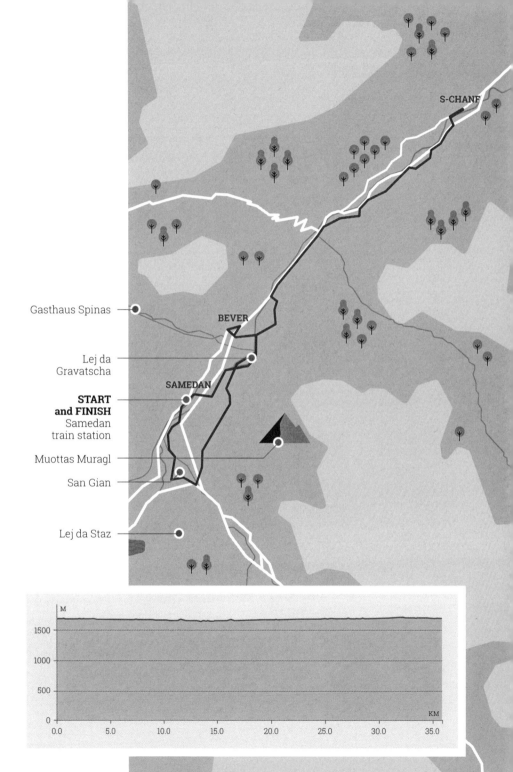

Gasthaus Spinas

Lej da
Gravatscha

**START
and FINISH**
Samedan
train station

Muottas Muragl

San Gian

Lej da Staz

S-CHANF

BEVER

SAMEDAN

M
1500
1000
500
0

0.0   5.0   10.0   15.0   20.0   25.0   30.0   35.0   KM

Route description

Cycle through the beauty of the Engadin Valley, with its clear, crisp light and magnificent mountains. Sit on a sunny terrace in the historic village of Bever. This is Graubünden at its best.

From Samedan, take regional cycling route #65 and go over to Bever at kilometer 3.7 (or kilometer 24.4 on the way back), then down the Inn River to S-chanf, where you'll turn around and head back the same way. At kilometer 28.1 the route splits. Take it to your left along the Flaz river to kilometer 32, where it turns right, past San Gian church. At kilometer 32.9, leave #65 to the right onto an agricultural road and follow it to kilometer 35.1. Turn left there onto the main road (Chaunt da San Bastiaun), right at the roundabout at kilometer 35.2 onto Via Retica and follow that 200 meters back to Samedan's train station.

Champesch

Along the way

Since the 1970s, the town planners of Bever have worked hard to preserve its historic center, designating a separate area for holiday apartment construction, which is heavily regulated in terms of design. The result is a quiet village of about 600 residents (and, according to its official website, 283 cows) who live in traditionally painted houses, many of which have been renovated in detail. Take a stroll through its beautiful lanes – and bring a good camera if the one in your phone is lacking.

A nice add-on from Bever is a ride up its side valley to the *Gasthaus* in Spinas. Just under four kilometers long with a gradual 109-meter elevation, it's a popular Sunday destination for hikers and cyclists.

If you love a gorgeous view, take the funicular up to Muottas Muragl, where on a clear day you can see St. Moritz, Sils Maria and all the way to Maloja. There's a hotel and restaurant with a panorama terrace at the top.

The small, 15th-century San Gian church outside Celerina has colorful wooden ceilings and frescoes depicting the lives of saints. The missing spire burnt down in 1682, when it was struck by lightning.

See how Engadin aristocrats lived from the 16th century onwards at Chesa Planta, the historical museum in Samedan. Chesa Planta is also a cultural center for Romansh music, literature and art, hosting regular events.

Bever

Cafés and restaurants are mostly collected in the towns and villages along the way, with a few destination restaurants here and there. Expect to find the specialties of the region in pretty much all of them (see below).

Lej da
Gravatscha

There are some picnic areas and spots off the trail to spread a blanket. Keep any eye out for signs telling you not to enter the fields and water systems surrounding Lej da Gravatscha (Lake Gravatscha) nature preserve.

Try classic Graubünden specialties like *Bündner Nusstorte* (filled with caramelized walnuts), *Engadiner Torte* (butter cream torte topped with a Florentine cover), *Bündnerfleisch* (air-dried beef), *Capuns* (dumplings with dried meat such as *Salsiz* or *Bündnerfleisch* wrapped in Swiss chard, cooked in milk and bouillon) or *Pizokel* (buckwheat dumplings with cheese). The last two come in all kinds of variations, so try them at more than one location if you have time.

This is not a big outdoor swimming region. The Inn River is cold, shallow and lined with rocks, although that makes it good for dangling hot feet into. The Lej da Gravatscha is part of a nature preserve, with no swimming allowed. The good news is that there are many natural hot springs here, with thermal baths and spas all over.

The Mineralbad & Spa Samedan is extraordinary in that the baths and steam rooms are distributed over five floors built over the source of its sulphuric hot springs. You move up from one bath to the next through rooms completely covered in glazed tiling (underwater too), each in a different color. The last pool is outside on the roof.

If you have time to go a bit farther, aim for Lej da Staz (Lake Staz), a beautiful small lake in the woods, with an alpine meadow, a small beach, a pier, a swimming raft and a playground. The water is warmer than in the larger Engadine lakes (which means it rises merely to about 20 C in the middle of summer). There are also changing rooms and fire pits for barbecues. The lake is 100 meters up from San Gian Church. Take the Via Dimlej from there or hoist your bike onto a train in Celerina to St. Moritz, then cycle over along the other end of Via Dimlej to Lej da Staz and back down to San Gian Church afterwards.

The Ovaverva Pool Spa & Sports Centre St. Moritz has four indoor pools (bathing, lengths, diving, wading) with slides and a large outdoor lounging pool with jets and other water features.

The larger hotels in Celerina, Pontresina and St. Moritz have pools and spas available to non-guests for a fee (some are subject to a membership, so be prepared). Children are often limited to an hour or two a day.

San Gian

As a major Swiss tourist area, you'll find accommodations in all price ranges, especially chalets, historic hotels and luxury properties.

GENEVA CIRCLE

Through high-tone suburbs out to the countryside

GENEVA

Geneva old town, CERN, United Nations

cafés, restaurants (international cuisine), picnic areas

Longeole pork sausage, *Cardon Genevois* vegetable, *Chèvre* fermenting wine with bubbles

Genève plage, Lake Geneva

all ranges

 START
Geneva

 FINISH
Geneva

 DISTANCE
35.16 km

 ELEVATION GAIN
0 m

 ASCENT
333 m

 DESCENT
333 m

 KID-FRIENDLY
yes

 TOURISM
geneve.com

 GPX TRACK
Flat Switzerland 33

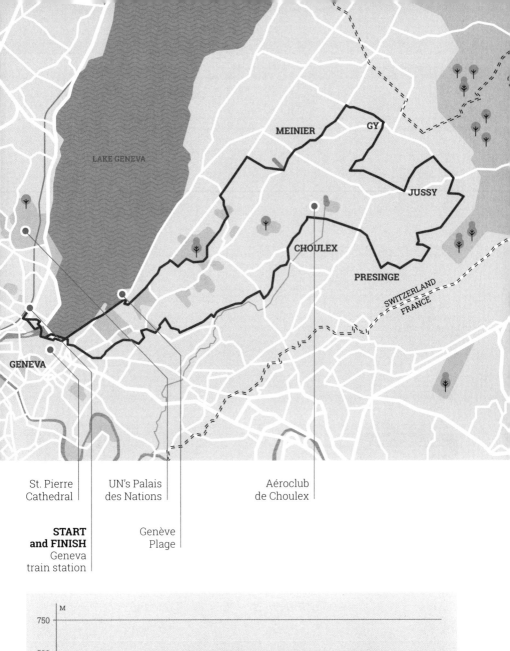

MEINIER

GY

JUSSY

LAKE GENEVA

CHOULEX

PRESINGE

SWITZERLAND
FRANCE

GENEVA

St. Pierre
Cathedral

UN's Palais
des Nations

Aéroclub
de Choulex

**START
and FINISH**
Geneva
train station

Genève
Plage

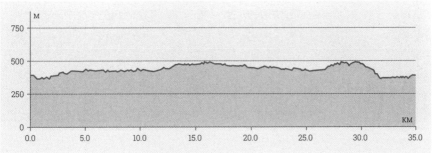

Route description

The quiet streets of one of Geneva's most exclusive suburbs lead out to the countryside, where you'll sometimes be sharing the road with young women on horses. Stop at the top of the route and admire the fabulous view: out over Lake Geneva on one side and the mountains of French Savoy on the other.

Follow regional cycling route #46 from Geneva's main train station (Cointrin). At kilometer 1.7, turn right onto Rue de la Scie, then left onto Rue François Versonnex. Turn left again onto Avenue de la gare des Eaux-Vives and follow #171 until kilometer 26.2, where you continue straight along Route de la Capite for 1.2 km, then turn left onto Chemin de la Messin, picking up #171 again. At kilometer 30.9, take Rampe de Cologny down to the lake and turn left onto the bike lane on waterfront on Quai Gustave-Ador. It's best to get off and use the crosswalk; the quay can be very busy. From there, follow #46 back to the train station.

Along the way

Climb up the hill to Geneva's old town, which is filled with restaurants, galleries and high-end shops. Maison Tavel takes you through the history of urban life over Geneva's last 1,000 years, the tower of St. Pierre Cathedral – the base of Protestant reformer Jean Calvin – offers a breathtaking view over the city. In the other direction, Promenade de la Treille looks out onto the city's university district and down onto the lush Parc des Bastions. The charming Place du Bourg-de-Four is a popular place for an outdoor meal or drink.

The CERN particle accelerator facilities are available to researchers from all around the world and they are open to the public as well. Its most famous installation is the Large Hadron Collider, which circles underground for 27 km through Switzerland and France. CERN's free tours present physics in such a way that you're sure you've understood everything when you come out. Cycle 7.4 km from Geneva's main train station along Route de Meyrin to CERN's visitor center. There is a separate bike lane, but it's busy and not scenic, so better yet, take tram 18 from the train station to the CERN terminus. Tours must be booked in advance.

The UN's Palais des Nations is sure to make you feel small. From the long row of flags and huge gates of its entrance off the Place des Nations through to the Cour d'Honneur in front of the Assembly Hall, the imposing architecture reflects the scale of the work being done inside. Tours must be booked in advance here as well.

Pressy

Food options are international and cover all price ranges in Switzerland's second-largest city. Thanks to the many parks throughout the city and along Lake Geneva, there's always a bench or lawn to have a picnic on. Supermarkets abound as well.

Specialties to try or take home are *Longeole* pork sausage with fennel, *Cardon Genevois* (a spikey vegetable reminiscent of artichokes often pickled or baked into casseroles), Chèvre, also called *champagne de paysan* (farmer's champagne) made of fermenting white wine, rice flour, dextrose vanilla and schnaps. It looks a bit like goat's milk, hence the name, but is bubbly like champagne.

The private Château du Crest

Geneve Plage

More recreational park than just a place to go swimming, Genève Plage is a complex directly on the lake that offers multiple ways to indulge your inner mermaid, with three pools (bathing, lengths, wading, 9-meter slide, beach with diving tower, lawns and shade trees, pebble beach, inflatable rafts).

There is a small beach at kilometer 27.1 with free access to the lake.

As an international city, Geneva offers all price ranges for accommodations, with a large selection of luxury hotels.

HELVETIQ publishing is supported by the Swiss Federal Office of Culture with a structural grant for the years 2021-2025.

Flat Switzerland
A fun cycling guide

Katrin Gygax
Illustrations: Elżbieta Kownacka
Photography: all photos copyright Katrin Gygax, except page 14 (shutterstock/swissdrone), page 50 bottom (shutterstock/Bee Bonnet), page 94–95 (shutterstock/Altrendo images) Shutterstock
Typesetting and layout: Elżbieta Kownacka
Editor: Richard Harvell
Proofreader: Karin Waldhauser

ISBN: 978-3-907293-67-6
First Edition: April 2022
Deposit copy in Switzerland: April 2022
Printed in the Czech Republic

www.helvetiq.com